NOTORIOUS NASHVILLE

SCOUNDRELS, ROGUES & OUTLAWS

BRIAN ALLISON

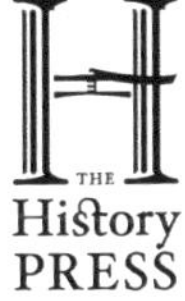

Published by The History Press
Charleston, SC
www.historypress.com

First published 2019

Manufactured in the United States

ISBN 9781467141246

Library of Congress Control Number: 2018963527

CONTENTS

ACKNOWLEDGEMENTS

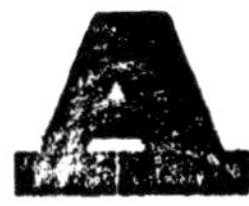

As always, a project like this takes many helping hands, and my sincere thanks go out to all who made it possible. First off, of course, are Chad Rhoad, Jonny Foster, Crystal Murray and the rest of The History Press, who have been so supportive of this and other projects. Thanks for giving me a platform to share these stories with others.

Also deserving of my thanks are the libraries and other institutions such as the Tennessee State Library and Archives and the Nashville Public Library, as well as Ken Fieth and his crew at the Metro Archives, Claire Horton at the Indiana State Archives and Elizabeth Odle at the Nashville Room.

I'm stunned by the generosity of many of the other authors and researchers who agreed to help me even when they didn't have to. Some of the leading experts on the Wild Bunch took the time to discuss Annie Rogers's story with me, especially Dan Buck, Sylvia Lynch, Donna Ernst, Donna Donnell, Wayne Kindred and Mark Smokov. I've been a fan of your work for years, and it was a thrill to kick ideas around with you all. Through their combined efforts, I believe that one day soon the mystery about who she was and where she ended up will finally be solved.

To the very dedicated local researchers and authors around me, my thanks as well. Tom Vickstrom shared his incredible knowledge about the Hermitage Hotel. Elizabeth Goetsch gave her valuable insight into the city's past. And Nikki Nelson Hicks helped me dissect several of the cases and gave me new theories to pursue.

Then there were the property owners who allowed me to tramp across their yards and intrude on their privacy in order to visit and photograph some of the scenes of these long-ago events. Martin Wiley, Nancy Yonko and others, thank you for your time. I appreciate your kindness and hospitality.

To my family and friends, thank you for putting up with all the nonsense that goes into writing one of these things. I know it can be a pain sometimes.

To those who just enjoy hidden places, unsolved mysteries and obscure history, I thank you for sharing an interest and giving me an excuse to explore the sometimes murky past of the city I call home.

And finally, to you, the reader. Thank you for picking this up, and I hope you enjoy it. If you have half as much fun reading it as I did writing it, then it's all worthwhile.

INTRODUCTION

Greetings, and welcome to Nashville, Tennessee.

In the past few years, it's become one of the hottest tourist spots in the country, with tens of thousands of visitors swarming in every summer in search of country music, hot chicken, good barbecue and cold beer. Go downtown on a raucous Saturday night (if you dare), and you'll see a press of literally thousands of people roaming the sidewalks at all hours while pedal taverns glide by, full of partygoers shouting the infamous "woo-hoo" that some locals have come to dread. It's a place where the party never seems to stop.

Of course, that's the Nashville of the guidebooks. That's the vacation getaway where the lights never go out. But like all cities, this one has some very dark alleys in its past, and to truly get to know a place, you sometimes have to venture away from the light.

Nashville is a historic city, and for those who want to know more, there is a wide selection of attractions on offer. There are the old antebellum houses and Civil War battlefields surrounding the city, along with sites that talk about the early settlers and Native American presence here. Downtown tours point out the few remaining historical buildings, and a state-of-the-art State Museum is about to open as of this writing, with artifacts from ancient Mississippian bowls to the banners of suffragists who won the right to vote in 1920. Another museum tells the story of the music scene that put the city on the map in the first place. All of these experiences will introduce you to Nashville's colorful native sons and daughters—presidents, politicians, soldiers, musicians and settlers who left a positive mark on the city.

This book is about people whose contribution to the narrative was a bit more dubious.

In the following pages, we're going to look at the city that once was and hear some of the stories that locals once only whispered about. It seems that just about everyone loves a good mystery, and there are several on offer here. The stories are true, but many of them are not very well known today, even among longtime residents. In these pages, you'll meet some of the more prominent miscreants who once strode across the stage. Jesse James, John Dillinger, the Wild Bunch and other semi-legendary figures in the nation's folklore—all of them passed through or called the city home at one time or another, and Nashville played a surprisingly prominent role in their legends.

You'll also get a look at some of the more mysterious doings that captivated the city from its founding up until 1940, such as a prisoner who seemed to pull an absolutely perfect escape, only to turn up in a shocking manner twenty years later, and a well-respected woman who gunned a man down in broad daylight and ended up paying for the crime in a most curious fashion. There are mysterious murders that went unsolved, along with seemingly innocent people accused of shocking crimes. Some of the places you'll visit within, such as Union Station, the Tennessee State Prison or the Hermitage Hotel, are still standing today. Others, like the long-forgotten gallows field, have been completely obliterated—perhaps understandably.

This is a book for those who like to explore the forgotten ends of history, for those who love a good mystery and for those who want to hear about characters on the fringes of society whose stories don't often make it into the record.

Nearly 700,000 people live here today, but whether you were born here or you've just arrived, this book will take you on a tour of the back alleys of centuries past. We're going back to before Nashville was Music City, USA, to see a side of the town where "decent folks" once feared to tread. So settle into your favorite chair, turn down the lights and get comfortable. It should be an interesting journey, so let's get started.

CHAPTER 1

UNTIL YOU ARE DEAD

Nashville is a city of secrets and hides them well. Oftentimes the most unremarkable neighborhoods were once the scene of life-and-death drama, and many modern residents would probably be surprised to find out what once occurred where their homes or businesses now stand. So it should come as no surprise that a quiet side street studded with modern businesses stands on the location of one of the most infamous sites in the city's history: the public gallows field. As is always the case, many sad spectacles once took place here, but arguably the most dramatic was a quartet of executions that took place in the winter of 1843.

At that time, hanging was still a public affair carried out before large crowds—part moral lesson and part entertainment. Nashville was no stranger to the gallows. The first recorded hanging in town took place on December 29, 1802, when Henry Beeler and Samuel Carman were executed for horse theft and larceny, respectively. Records are incomplete, but in the following three decades, at least ten men would be put to death for crimes ranging from horse theft to murder.

In those days, the community was steadily growing, but it was still a small town. There were fewer than eight thousand residents in 1842, and unlike some river towns, it was a relatively dull place. Violent crime was comparatively rare. For those who had the sense not to go gambling and drinking down in "Vinegar Hill," life was largely safe and steady. That's probably why the news that no fewer than four men were on trial for their lives before the Supreme Court in December of that year grabbed the public imagination in the way that it did.

The quartet at the center of this drama was from various walks of life. Only one was a local, and he seems to be the only one whose story generates any kind of sympathy today. His case would be the first to come before the court.

His name was Jacob, and he was born into slavery and grew into a physically powerful young man. From all accounts, he had an independent streak along with a short temper born of the constant constraints of bondage, and that's what ended up costing him his life.

Jacob lived on Granny White Pike at the plantation of forty-three-year-old Robert Bradford, and there was constant friction between the planter and the slave. After a minor argument, Jacob ran away for a few days, and when he returned, Bradford was determined to "correct" him—a polite euphemism for whipping. On August 17, 1840, Robert Bradford and his brother Frederick confronted and attempted to beat Jacob, who drew a hidden butcher knife and struck back blindly. Apparently, he only meant to clear a path through his assailants, but the knife struck home in Bradford's side, inflicting a fatal wound. Jacob went on the lam and avoided capture for several months, but eventually he was arrested, tried and convicted of murder.

There seems to have been quite a bit of support for Jacob outside Tennessee. Indeed, a sympathetic abolitionist newspaper in Maine caused some controversy by running the story of Bradford's killing under the headline "Served Him Right!"[1] Jacob's attorney appealed his conviction to the Supreme Court in what became a landmark case regarding slave-master relations. Remarkably, the three justices ruled that slaves were similar to students or apprentices and that masters were allowed to punish them in "moderation," though they didn't define what constituted moderation. They ruled that a master did not have the right to kill a slave, and conceivably, a slave could kill an owner in self-defense in such cases. Unfortunately for Jacob, the court also decided there was no proof that the Bradfords had intended to kill him, and therefore his action could not be considered self-defense.

On the cold morning of January 28, 1843, Jacob was hauled to the public gallows, riding in a cart and seated on his own coffin. There was a large crowd of spectators, and he made a short speech before he died, confessing that Bradford hadn't been his only victim. Seven years earlier, he had killed another slave, for which an innocent man had been condemned and hanged. Witness James Thomas had attended this earlier execution and later vividly recalled how, just before he died, the condemned man had proclaimed

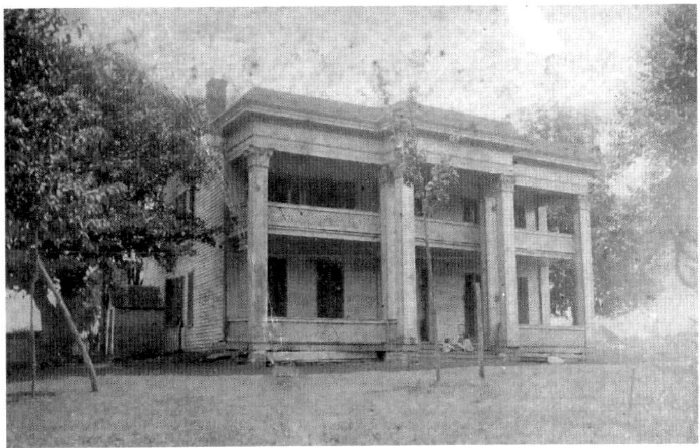

Photograph of the Bradford plantation house on Granny White Pike. It was near this spot that the tragedy between Jacob and Robert Bradford occurred. *Courtesy Metro Nashville Archives.*

from the gallows that they were "shedding innocent blood."[2] It appears that Jacob had avoided punishment by remaining silent on that occasion, but his reprieve proved temporary. Now he stood in the exact same spot where the victim of his silence had died, ready to meet the same end.

The turnout at his death was so large in part because slave owners considered hangings like this to be object lessons. Thomas recalled that many planters made their slaves attend hangings to "go and learn what they might be brought to" if they disobeyed in the future.[3]

Jacob's execution was the opening round. The gallows was left standing afterward, and there would be a need for it very soon. Evidently wishing to save effort and time, the state decided to review the three other capital cases at the same time, and if the convictions were upheld, all three were to be hanged simultaneously. This would be the first triple hanging in the city's history, and the residents flocked to the morbid spectacle.

One of the prisoners was represented by a silver-tongued attorney named Milton Andrews Haynes. Sensing the public interest in the case, he decided to cash in by publishing a small pamphlet to tell the stories of those on trial. The result, *Lives and Confessions of Zebediah Payne, Willis Green Carroll, and Archibald Kerby* [*sic*], is the earliest surviving "true crime" book from Tennessee. Remarkably, Haynes allowed the three doomed men to pen their own biographies, giving us an unusually vivid look at their lives.

Not that any of those lives had much to recommend them. The three men were not actually from Nashville but from surrounding counties. Their transgressions had been heinous indeed. Green Carroll was arguably the least appealing of the lot, convicted at Gallatin, Tennessee, of shooting Reverend Isaac Lindsey in the back and robbing him of $102.

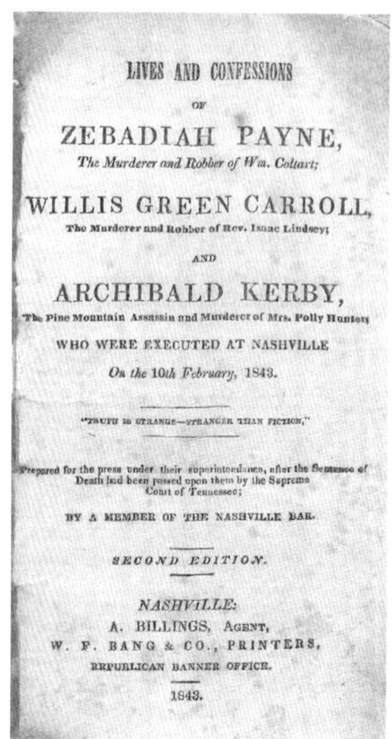

LIVES AND CONFESSIONS

OF

ZEBADIAH PAYNE,

The Murderer and Robber of Wm. Coltart;

WILLIS GREEN CARROLL,

The Murderer and Robber of Rev. Isaac Lindsey;

AND

ARCHIBALD KERBY,

The Pine Mountain Assassin and Murderer of Mrs. Polly Hunter;

WHO WERE EXECUTED AT NASHVILLE

On the 10th February, 1843.

"TRUTH IS STRANGE—STRANGER THAN FICTION,"

Prepared for the press under their superintendance, after the Sentence of Death had been passed upon them by the Supreme Court of Tennessee;

BY A MEMBER OF THE NASHVILLE BAR.

SECOND EDITION.

NASHVILLE:

A. BILLINGS, AGENT,

W. F. BANG & CO., PRINTERS,

REPUBLICAN BANNER OFFICE.

1843.

Three convicted murderers were destined to meet their fate together on Nashville's gallows. This small pamphlet published at the time gives a detailed look at the lives of the condemned men. *Courtesy Tennessee State Library and Archives.*

He ran to Van Buren, Arkansas, before being arrested and returned for trial. Surly and cold, he said little and wouldn't even confirm his age or background. He offered only the usual denials that he was guilty of anything.

Then there was Zeb Payne. He was far more charming and possessed a "manly beauty…[and] ingenious countenance,"[4] but that was the sum of his redeeming qualities. Only twenty-two, he was from Bedford County and had been tried for cutting the throat of a young traveling companion named William Coltart near Roseville before skipping out for the Republic of Texas. At the time, Texas was an independent nation, and many wanted men sought sanctuary there. Payne felt secure enough to travel under his real name, but unfortunately for him, his new country had a strong extradition treaty with the United States. He made no friends among his new neighbors when he joined a local gang of outlaws and helped them commit at least one more murder. Before long, Tennessee bounty hunters had arrived at San Augustine and arrested him, taking him home for trial.

The most prominent of the three was Archy Kirby, a forty-six-year-old farmer who hailed from near Sparta in White County, where he was already notorious as the "Pine Mountain Assassin." He'd come by the nickname the hard way—incredibly, he'd been in this same position before.

Back in 1830, he had sunk a tomahawk into the neck of a neighbor named Peter Elrod, robbing him and leaving his body near a waterfall on top of Pine Mountain, known locally as the "Hell Hole." Tried and convicted, his case had been appealed in 1837 to the Supreme Court, which had overturned his conviction, citing procedural errors by the lower court. Needless to say, the decision was received poorly in White County. His own lawyer, Sam Turney, had remarked at the time, "You're as guilty as hell, and if you ever murder again, I'll volunteer to hang you!"[5] Now here was Kirby once more before the Supreme Court, and tradition has it that among the spectators in the crowd was Turney, determined to offer his services to the state. There is no word on whether it took him up on his kind offer.

This time, Kirby was accused of an even more cold-blooded act. On the night of May 11, 1842, a sniper took aim through the window of a cabin near Sparta and fired a rifle ball that struck Mrs. Polly Hunter in the throat, killing her almost instantly. The victim was a widow of around sixty years of age, and the motive for her murder was unclear, although there seems to have been a property dispute between herself and her son-in-law. Kirby was soon arrested, suspected of being a hit man hired by the son-in-law to get her out of the way.

A chain of circumstantial evidence soon tied him to the crime. He had been seen in the neighborhood that day, over twenty-five miles from his house, with no convincing reason for being there. A witness saw him carrying the suspected murder weapon on the day of the killing, and a set of footprints was found in the mud near the window that looked very much like those made by Kirby's shoes. For the second time, he was convicted of murder and sentenced to death.

Milton Haynes was retained as his attorney for the appeals process, and he made a valiant effort. In an impassioned speech before the court, he questioned some of the witnesses' identifications of his client. He raised the possibility of other suspects who hadn't been properly investigated—most particularly, some of the slaves at Polly Hunter's place, who were under the mistaken impression that they would be freed in the case of her death. He called for a new trial on the basis of these doubts. The entirety of his speech was included in his pamphlet, and indeed, one suspects he did so to showcase his own eloquence.

In the end, it made little difference. While the court admitted that Haynes had spoken "earnestly and ingeniously,"[6] it nevertheless upheld the chain of evidence and saw no reason to overthrow it. The conviction was sustained, as were those of Carroll and Payne.

The courtroom was packed on the freezing morning of January 18, 1843, as the three prisoners were brought to the bar and their fates pronounced by Justice Nathan Green Sr. After summing up their cases and dwelling on their sins in great detail, Green advised them to spend their final days looking after their immortal souls, in "days of penitence" and "nights of devotion and prayer." He then pronounced the traditional sentence of death: "the judgment of the law is, that…Friday the 10th day of February…between the hours of 10 o'clock in the morning, and 2 o'clock in the evening, you be taken to the public gallows...and hung by the neck until you are DEAD. *And may God have mercy on your souls.*"[7]

The three were taken back to their cell in the jailhouse on Water Street, where they would have nearly a month to contemplate their fates. Hanging has never been a very efficient or clean method of execution, but in those days, it was an especially brutal practice. The "drop"—where the victim would fall several feet through a trapdoor—had not yet been adopted, so there was virtually no chance the neck would break. Instead, the condemned was "turned off" a ladder or cart and left to slowly strangle, jerking in agony until unconsciousness overcame him. This "gallows jig" was considered one of the morbid attractions by the crowd of spectators. Often the hangman would have to grab the victim's legs and pull downward to try to hasten his or her end. Even in the best circumstances, it was an incredibly gruesome business, and it is evident that the gravity of the situation weighed heavily on the minds of the prisoners.

Haynes asked them to write their life stories, and Payne and Kirby both complied. Their efforts were remarkably literate—if one-sided—proclaiming their innocence to the end. Payne was especially florid, quoting Shakespeare and several poets. However, offsetting these claims of innocence, Haynes also included a jailhouse confession from another prisoner who said that Payne had admitted to killing William Coltart after all. The confession is full of grotesque detail that gives it the ring of truth, claiming that Payne said he'd clubbed his victim with a pistol before setting on him with a knife. Coltart put up a fight, and Payne jabbed him a few dozen times in the chin, trying to get at his throat, eventually breaking the blade of his weapon. Seizing the broken blade, he then forced it into the young man's throat with his bare hands, killing him. For this effort, Payne managed to score "only about $60 in Alabama money"[8]—paper bills practically worthless in Tennessee.

Carroll's literary efforts were limited to a disturbing and jumbled couple of paragraphs, wherein he claimed that the ghost of his victim entered his cell window every evening and hovered around him, "gently touching my eyeballs with his finger."[9] He vowed to himself return as a ghost and haunt the jail after death. Indeed, the whole essay is unsettling and leaves a modern reader wondering if he wasn't truly mentally ill.

The day before the execution saw some excitement at the jail. After handing their manuscripts to Haynes, Kirby and Payne asked him to make one last appeal to Governor "Lean Jimmy" Jones on their behalf. Told that this was impossible, the two men broke down into tears, but eventually they pulled themselves together and asked to be baptized by Reverend John Berry

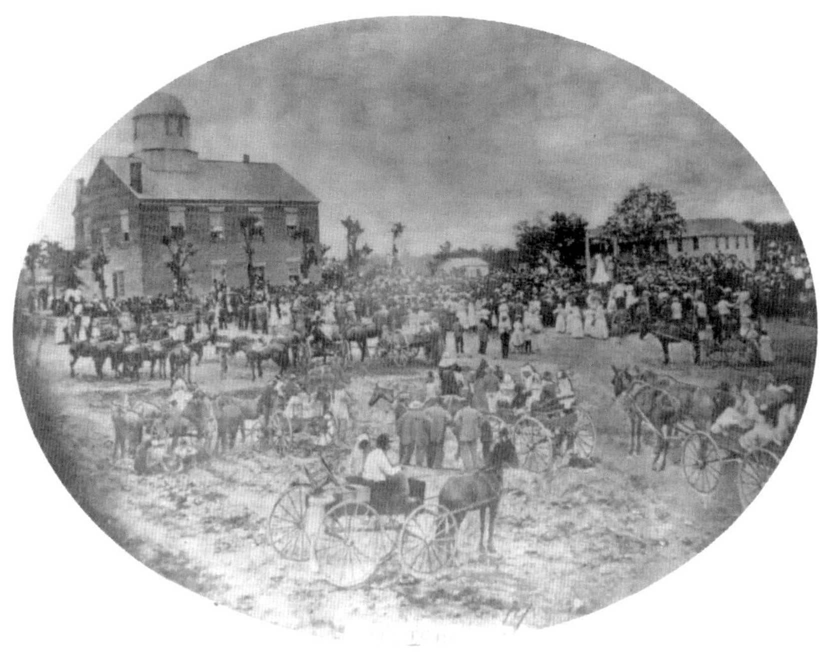

No cameras were around to record Nashville's triple hanging, but the scene would have been very similar to this scene of a hanging at Smithville in 1872. *Library of Congress.*

McFerrin. Carroll, a professed Catholic, spent the day with Bishop Richard Pius Miles, making his confession and taking the Eucharist in his cell.

But he and Payne had no intention of going quietly. They pooled their funds and approached an African American man who worked in the jail, asking him to purchase some laudanum and smuggle it in to them so they could quietly commit suicide before they swung. The man refused, so late that night, the pair took a more direct tack. Tying cords to a peg and a nail in their cells, they tried to strangle themselves. During the attempt, the peg broke, and Carroll hit the ground with enough force to wake Kirby. Seeing what they were up to, he intervened and somehow managed to talk them into giving up their efforts.

At daylight, the men changed into long white smocks—their grave clothes—and the final round of visitors came by to bid them farewell. Family and friends came to see Kirby and Payne, along with dignitaries and curiosity seekers. Carroll remained aloof, speaking only to Bishop Miles. A relative attempted to talk with him, reminding him of how freely he used to converse with her. Carroll sneered at her and responded, "I'll take it out in thinking."[10]

Finally, at a word from the jailer, the three men entered a large cart in the courtyard for the ride to the gallows. Surrounded by the local militia companies—the Harrison Guards and the Straightouts—in their finest uniforms, the cart jerked along College Street (now Third Avenue), past the University of Nashville campus and toward the public commons.

Citizens lined the sidewalks watching the three doomed men go by. The excitement of the moment was too much for one woman along the route. Nancy Taylor was watching from the window of her residence when she suddenly collapsed from "congestion of the brain"—probably a stroke. She was carried to bed, but nothing could be done, and she died two days later. She was forty-six years old.

Finally, the cart halted under the crossbeam of the gallows where Jacob had died just a few weeks before. About one thousand people gathered on the surrounding high ground to watch. Reverend Alexander Little Page Green (who later founded Vanderbilt University) delivered a brief but moving sermon before the ropes were fastened around the men's necks. They were then asked if they had any final words.

Predictably, Carroll said nothing. Payne made a short statement in which he maintained his innocence but said, "Since the laws of my country have doomed me to die, I yield up my life cheerfully." Kirby, though, was too angry to be magnanimous. "I am to be *murdered* this day for the *murder* of Polly Hunter," he shouted, "a woman I have not seen in 26 or 27 years!" The caps were then drawn over their heads, and Kirby leaned down to say farewell to a relative. As his head disappeared from sight, an angry murmur went through the crowd; some thought he had received a last-minute reprieve and was stepping down from the cart.

Without warning, the signal was given, and the cart trundled away, leaving all three men jerking and struggling in midair. So unexpected was the move that it caught Payne's sister off guard, and she let out a bloodcurdling shriek that hung for several moments over the suddenly hushed crowd.[11]

After a long while, their bodies finally stopped jerking, and the spectators dispersed. Friends and family were weeping and grim-faced, while others were actually laughing and cracking jokes as they moved along, much to the disgust of an observer. Still wrapped in their shrouds, the dead were unceremoniously bundled into boxes for burial. Whether they lie in the nearby City Cemetery or were returned to their families is unknown today.

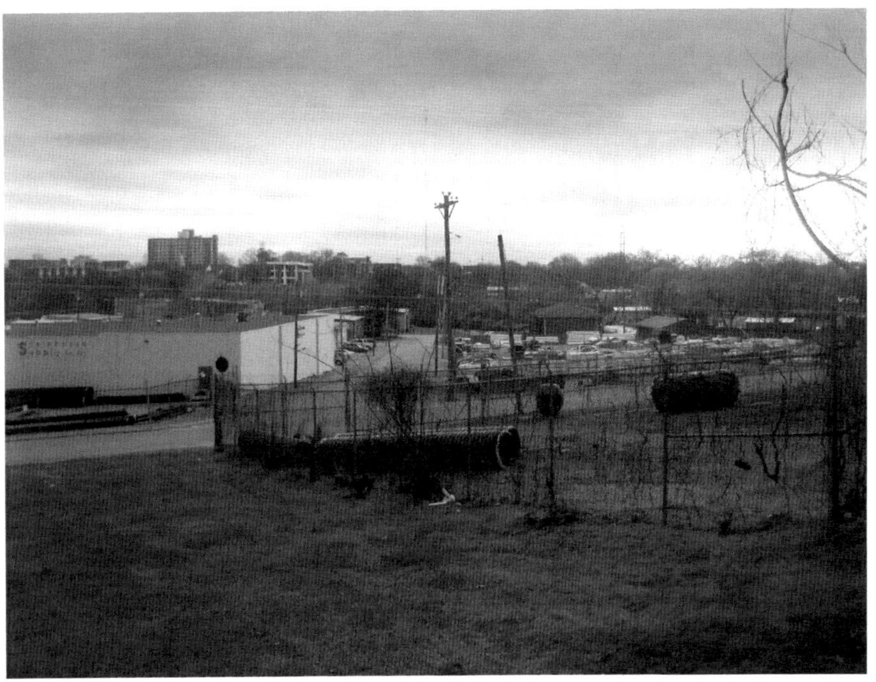

Nashville's hanging field today. No reminders remain of the neighborhood's turbulent past. The gallows were erected near present-day Lewis Street, about the middle of this photograph. *Author's photograph.*

With that, the sorry spectacle came to an end, but it wouldn't be the last of these tragedies to play out on the spot. The old gallows field remained in use for years until the last hanging was carried out here in 1874. After that, the law changed, and future hangings were to be carried out in private behind the walls of the jail on Front Street. By that time, the Rock City Paper Mill had taken over the old gallows field, and industry rapidly eradicated most of the green space in the neighborhood, blotting out all memory of the grim scenes once enacted here. In truth, it was a history nobody wanted to remember.

Whether or not Green Carroll was able to make good his threat to return to haunt the living is unknown, but if he did, he would hardly be alone. Ghosts of Nashville's past are often just beneath the fabric of the modern city, as we shall soon see...

CHAPTER 2

CANE RIDGE FEUD

Turning south on Old Hickory Boulevard from Bell Road, a modern traveler will soon leave the urban sprawl of Antioch behind and find a reminder of the rural countryside that was once so typical of the areas outside the city. It makes for a serene and peaceful setting today, but it wasn't always so. A century and a half ago, these farm fields and wood lots served as the backdrop to a saga of murder and revenge that could have come straight out of Shakespearian drama.

In 1874, Cane Ridge was a sparsely settled district of log homes and small farms straddling the Davidson-Williamson County line. It was far removed from the modern conveniences of the city beyond the lifeline provided by the tracks of the Nashville and Chattanooga (N&C) Railroad. Since well before the Civil War, the family of John G. Briley had made their home on a modest farm here. They were prominent and law-abiding citizens; in addition to his carpentry business, Briley served as a justice of the peace. Together with his wife, Sarah, he made a relatively comfortable home, raising a total of three daughters and four sons.

His sons grew up to be popular and outgoing young men, but as in any community, rivalries were bound to spring up. Just why the Briley boys fell out with the Bates family is unclear today, but it soon developed into a serious conflict.

Robert Page Bates was twenty-one, a son of John and Mary Bates, who lived in the far western part of the county. Described as "a tall, well-built young man," he had acquired something of a reputation as a fighter who

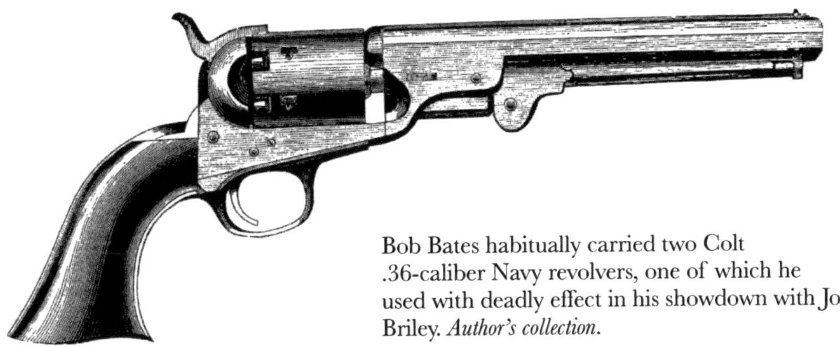

Bob Bates habitually carried two Colt .36-caliber Navy revolvers, one of which he used with deadly effect in his showdown with Jo Briley. *Author's collection.*

habitually went armed with a brace of Colt Navy revolvers. According to his version of events, the bad blood started when he and Bob Briley both worked for the Nashville and Northwestern Railroad. A dispute between them ended in fisticuffs, and of course, both claimed that the other one lost the fight. The two managed to steer clear of each other for some time, but on the night of January 30, 1874, they collided at a country dance.

A neighbor named Payne threw a ball and invited all the young folks of the district to come and enjoy themselves. By all accounts it was a fine night, though cold. His house, a double-pen log cabin, swayed under the thud of dancing feet while hands clapped time and the fiddles squealed. Bob Bates and his older brother Ben were in attendance when suddenly Bob, Jim and Joel Briley sauntered into the room. The trio had been out fox hunting and had decided to stop in and join the fun.

Bates's friend Ferd Morton gave him a heads-up, and there seems to have been some sort of verbal exchange between Bates and Bob Briley, but the two Bobs were separated, and it appeared to be over. The dancers began prepping themselves for a new set, and Joel Briley asked a young lady in attendance to dance with him. At that moment, Bates appeared and addressed her, saying, "I believe this is our set." Briley disagreed, but Bates turned to the girl. "I will leave it to the lady," he said, and Briley agreed. After a pause, she made her choice. "Jo Briley," she said, "it is yours."[12] He squired her onto the floor while Bates withdrew, claiming he would dance with someone else.

Instead, he made his way through the crowd to the "dog-trot" of the cabin, where his father and brother were talking. Ben was holding his revolvers for him, but when Bob made out that he was facing trouble with the Briley crowd, Ben handed one over. Now armed, Bob Bates stepped back into the room.

A young woman saw him coming and screamed that a man was about to shoot someone. Everyone froze as Bob Bates stepped up to Jo Briley and made the announcement, "Look a-here! I'm going to shoot....I'm going to kill somebody!" Briley was either very brave or just didn't take him seriously. Making no attempt to defend himself, he simply said, "Well, shoot then."[13]

Bates didn't need another invitation. He raised the pistol to within inches of Briley's chest and fired a single round that went straight through his heart. Briley shouted, "Oh, my God! Oh, my God!" in disbelief before crumpling to the floor. Within minutes, he was dead.

The bystanders were still frozen with shock, and Bates raised his pistol, shouting, "Everybody—stand back. The first one that lays a hand on me I will serve in the same way!" Understandably, nobody moved to stop him as he walked into the yard. Looking around, Bates shouted, "There is one more of the family I want to kill!" But look as Bates might, Bob Briley had the sense to stay hidden in the house. Finally, the young gunman retrieved his horse and his other revolver and rode off into the freezing darkness.

Jo Briley had celebrated his seventeenth birthday only three weeks before he was killed. His body was carried back to his father's house for burial in the family cemetery. The entire family was heartbroken, but none took it as hard as James Porter Briley, Jo's sixteen-year-old brother. To any who would listen, he vowed that one day he would kill his brother's murderer.

Before that happened, the State of Tennessee stepped in. Four days after the killing, Governor John C. Brown issued a proclamation calling for Bates's arrest, offering $300 reward for his capture. Two weeks later, there was a stir when a man answering his description was arrested in Wayne County, but it turned out to be mistaken identity. The arrested man was Tillman Haynes, who was wanted for murdering a Confederate veteran near Franklin a few weeks earlier. The real Bob Bates had vanished, and months went by with no sign of him.

Then on March 18, a Memphis police detective named Harry Cranmer rode into the farmyard of a Dr. Eddings near Bartlett and identified himself as a county assessor. He asked the doctor's newest farmhand to accompany him to the barn in order to count some horses, but once inside, he pulled his pistol and said, "Mr. Bates, I have come to carry you to town....I am not an assassin, but a detective," adding that if the fugitive resisted, Cranmer would "be compelled to hurt." Wisely, Bates made no play, and Cranmer slapped the cuffs on him. By that evening, the fugitive was on a train heading for Nashville.[14]

He spoke freely about the affair, saying that the day after he killed Briley, he'd hidden in Mr. Crockett's barn at Brentwood but had been discovered by a farmhand the following morning and hopped a southbound train. He had ridden the rails as far as Decatur, Alabama, where he ran out of money and was forced to sell one of his pistols to a soldier. He hid in Arkansas for a while, "but not liking that country," he returned to Tennessee, where he hired on at Dr. Eddings's place. Not surprisingly, his version of events on the night of the killing was quite at odds with many other witnesses'. According to Bates, the three Briley boys had showed up intending to attack him and "break up" the dance. Of course, he didn't explain why they seemed more intent on dancing with the girls once they arrived. In his version, a drunk and crazy Jo Briley had tried to draw a gun only to have it snag in the lining of his pocket, forcing Bates to fire in self-defense. He boasted that it wasn't his first killing, saying, "I have killed two negroes in my life....I do not think much of killing negroes, and yet hate to take the life of a white man." He further hinted that he had something to do with the disappearance of several other African American men from his neighborhood.[15]

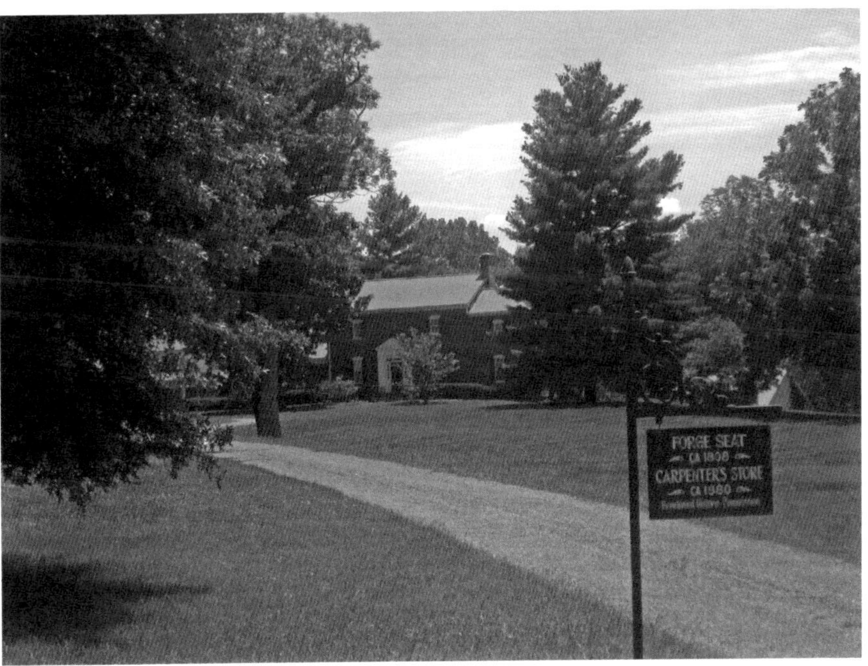

The Crockett home in Brentwood. Bates hid out in a nearby barn the night after he shot Briley before hopping a train to make his escape. *Author's photograph.*

The cocky young killer was put into the fetid confines of the county jail until his trial came up a year later. His mouth made him no friends in his new home, with one reporter claiming that "after two days of boasting, his fellow-prisoners grew tired of his talk, combined against him, and he now has but little to say."[16] Twelve months of jail time took the starch out of him, and he was far more subdued by the time he walked into Judge Frazier's courtroom on January 26, 1875, to stand trial for his life.

After two days of testimony, the jury members retired to deliberate. They were out three days in all before they returned with their verdict: guilty of murder in the second degree. Bates was given ten years and one day in prison.

Given the circumstances, the verdict was considered very light, but his counsel nonetheless applied for a new trial, and Bates returned to jail pending his appeal. He proved a remarkably quiet prisoner, so much so that when two jailbirds broke out on February 11, he remained in his cell and made no effort to join them. Nevertheless, his appeal failed, and in the spring of 1875, Bob Bates donned the black stripes and entered the dark and dangerous walls of the penitentiary.

He was put to work in the foundry, where he learned to be a molder. He kept to task and stayed out of trouble, earning a reduction of sentence of four years. In 1881, he finally walked out the front gate a free man. Drawing on his prison experience, he got a job with an iron foundry in town where he was known as a "good, quiet workman."[17] In 1883, he became engaged to Mollie Roberts, twelve years his junior, whom he planned to wed in November. The Bates who emerged from prison was a reformed man, far more mature and subdued than the wild young hothead who'd gone in.

It had been nine years, but the Briley boys had not forgotten. Jim Briley, now twenty-five and working as a freight conductor on the N&C, still maintained his vow to kill Bates. Word got around that trouble was brewing, and Bates began carrying a pistol just in case.

Yet months went by without incident. At one point, Bates even encountered Briley on the streets of Nashville, but instead of drawing on him, the younger man passed him without a word. Bates's guard relaxed somewhat, and on the afternoon of October 22, 1883, he decided to treat his fiancée by taking her to see Barrett's traveling circus.

The circus was always a draw, and Barrett's bunch made quite a spectacle as they camped in the Sulphur Spring bottom. The act included 125 trained horses, 40 trick ponies and exotic beasts such as an elephant and a herd of camels. Bates was in fine spirits as the afternoon performance

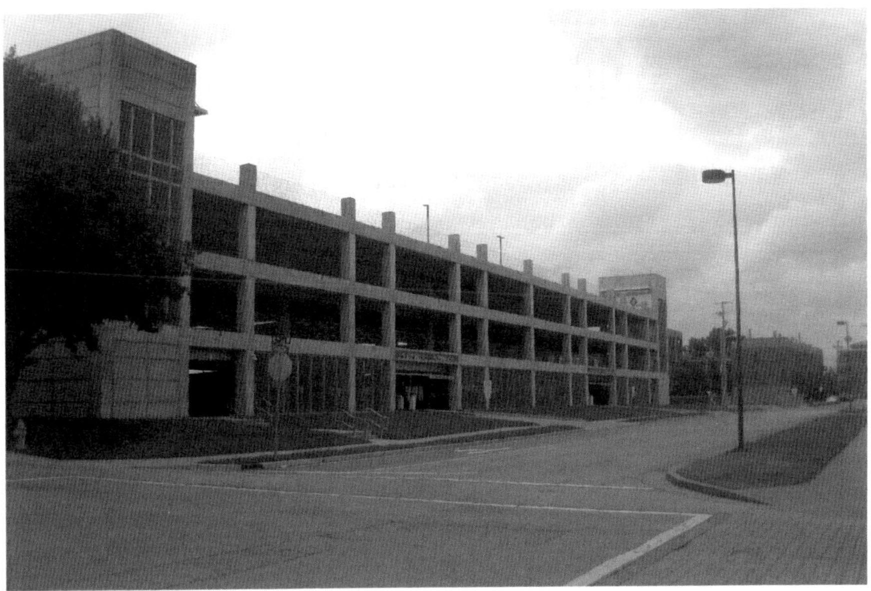

The corner of Fifth and Harrison today. This is the approximate location where Briley shot Bates in 1883. At the time this was the Sulphur Spring bottom where Barrett's circus had spread its canvas. *Author's photograph.*

wound down. The climax of the show was always the performing horses, and he asked Mollie if she cared to head down ringside to watch. She politely declined, preferring to keep her seat in the stands, so he went down alone and joined the spectators marveling at the whirling riders and prancing animals. He even lifted up a six-year-old girl and held her up on his shoulder so she could see better.

He seemed unaware of the cold gaze of Jim Briley just a few seats away. Without any fanfare, the young man stood up and pushed forward, drawing a .38 Smith & Wesson from his pants pocket. Yelling "Take that, damn you!" he stepped up to Bates, who had shifted the child to his other arm and was just turning away from him. Briley raised the pistol, shoved it just past the little girl's body and pulled the trigger.

There was panic at the sudden gunshot, and people scrambled to get away as Bates fell heavily to the ground, crying, "O Lordy!" He landed on several children, who screamed and crawled out from under him. The little girl he had been carrying was unharmed but naturally terrified.

The bullet had torn into Bates's hip, inflicting a debilitating but not fatal wound, and Briley elbowed his way through the terrified bystanders, cocking the pistol again while shouting, "Get up, you son of a bitch!"[18] Then he placed the muzzle against his victim's chest and fired again, scorching his shirt with burned powder. This time, the ball passed through the heart. Within minutes, Bob Bates was dead.

The scene was pure pandemonium by now as terrified patrons were "wildly tearing at the canvas" of the tent trying to get away. Two county constables and Officer J. Hadley Clack (a future police chief) were standing nearby when the shooting happened and grabbed the shooter's pistol hand. Briley offered no resistance and handed over his weapon.

With several hundred witnesses present, it was little wonder that Briley was immediately charged with murder. He retained Judge James M. Quarles as his attorney. The family was backing Jim to the hilt, as his new mouthpiece didn't come cheap. Quarles was a former U.S. representative and one of the most eminent lawyers in town. In an ironic twist of fate, he had also represented Bates nine years earlier when he was tried for killing Jo Briley.

He entered a plea of not guilty for his client, who was promptly deposited in the "Murderer's Cell" in the basement of the jail. That's where a reporter for the *American* found him and asked him for a statement. The reporter found him to be a bright young man with a blond mustache who displayed a rock-steady nerve. "I've hired Judge Quarles to do my talking," was all he would say and refused to discuss the matter further.[19]

His victim was laid to rest the next day at Mount Olivet Cemetery, attended by many friends and admirers. The local chapter of the Knights of Labor performed a graveside ceremony honoring their fallen brother.

Circuses of the time were noted for attracting a rowdy element, and violence was not uncommon. One local paper noted that "one never stops here without causing a row."[20] But this was different: a blood feud ending with a man shot dead with a child in his arms in front of hundreds of witnesses, including his own intended wife. It was Victorian melodrama at its finest, and the press were sharpening their pencils when Jim Briley entered the courthouse on October 30, 1883.

From the beginning, the public was captivated. Mollie Roberts was front and center, delivering an eyewitness account of her fiancé's shooting. Many commented on the dramatic way she laid it out before the jury, acting out the part of both shooter and victim. Witnesses established that the deceased was shot in the back and then shot once more while lying on the ground. Other testimony said that Bates had previously threatened Briley's life and habitually carried pistols. A "little brass pepperbox pistol" *was* found near the spot where Bates died, but it was unclear who dropped it, and at any rate, it was empty. The closing arguments were pure theater, with the defense maintaining Briley acted in defense of his life and the state calling it a cowardly and cold-blooded assassination.

The members of the jury got the case on a Saturday, and for three days they were deadlocked. Finally, they returned with a dramatic announcement. They were nine to three for acquittal and "would not agree if kept together until Christmas."[21] The judge reluctantly released Briley on $8,000 bond, and he went home the same day to his family. The state vowed that it would retry him very soon.

The railroad nearly saved them the trouble. On the night of January 26, 1884, four cars broke loose from a train going up Cumberland Mountain, smashing into a following locomotive and rolling down the mountainside. Conductor Jim Briley and his brother were on one of the cars and were thrown clear in the wreck. Incredibly, they were unhurt, and Jim lived to face his next day in court the following November.

For the most part, the testimony was the same, but new key witnesses were introduced, including Tom Roach, who testified that Briley shouted,

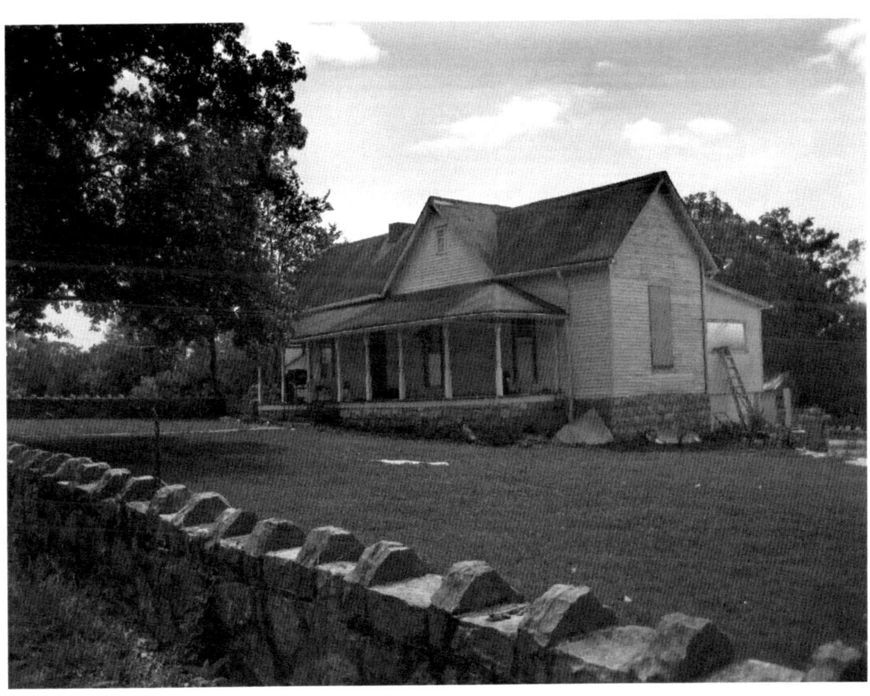

Years after the circus tragedy, Jim Briley's son Bob became the sheriff of Davidson County. He built this house around 1915. Legend has it that he used prisoners from the jail to build it. *Author's photograph.*

"You threatened my life!" before firing—a detail no other witness seemed to remember. Another recalled Briley telling him while Bates was in prison, "He [Briley] intended to kill Bates when he came out, and that he would kill him if he met him on the streets in his stripes."[22]

Once more, the opposing attorneys made their closing remarks. Once more, the jury members retired to deliberate. This time, they were back bright and early the following day. On November 29, 1884, they made their announcement: not guilty as charged in the indictment. The "long and weary" attempt to convict him was finally over, and James Briley was free to go.[23]

It was also the end of the vendetta. Briley had his revenge, and luckily for him, nobody came looking to even the score. Within a short time, the tragedies were forgotten. Briley lived quietly for the rest of his life, conducting a general store near his home on Cane Ridge and raising five sons. One of them, Robert, would go on to become the sheriff of Davidson County in 1926. At the time he died, the papers delicately avoided any mention of his youthful scrapes, saying that he was "a man of strong convictions, and a leader in the Christian church."[24] Of course, one hopes he later became familiar with a verse with which he seemed unacquainted in his youth: Romans 12:19, "Vengeance is mine; I will repay, saith the Lord."

Nashville often looks more at the future than the past, and this backcountry feud was strictly a local story, quickly forgotten. But even as that story was unfolding, the city was unknowingly playing host to a pair of notorious characters who were infamous nationwide and whose criminal deeds are still the stuff of legends.

CHAPTER 3

MR. WOODSON AND MR. HOWARD

Simply put, the James brothers were legends even in their own lifetimes. Lauded as heroes by some, called cutthroats by others, they were members of one of the first truly successful bank- and train-robbing gangs of the Old West. A century after their crime spree, author Peter Lyon summed up their outlaw career. Noting that Mrs. James wept at the graveside for her "generous, noble-hearted Jesse," he acidly commented that her boy was "the leader of a gang of comparably generous, noble-hearted thugs who, in fifteen years, held up eleven banks, seven trains, three stages, one county fair, and one payroll messenger, in the process… killing at least sixteen men. What the mothers of those sixteen said at their graves has not been recorded."[25]

They were products of the Civil War, and their escapades helped keep that conflict alive for twenty years after the Confederate surrender. Alexander Franklin James, the older of the two, was born on January 10, 1843, in Clay County, Missouri. His little brother Jesse Woodson James followed on September 5, 1847. Had the war not come along when it did, the bookish Frank (or "Buck," as he was known) might have become a schoolteacher. Jesse, pious and proper, was on his way to a quiet life as a Bible-thumping farmer.

But the war did come, and it visited a terrible devastation on the boys' home state. By the end of it, Missouri was overrun by thieves, guerrillas and bushwhackers of every stripe. The state was under the rule of martial law, and the James brothers were part of the reason why. Frank was the first into the saddle, riding with the vicious gang of bushwhackers led by William C. Quantrill, with whom he took part in the infamous massacre at Lawrence, Kansas, in which hundreds of men were killed.

Jesse stayed home at first, but when he was beaten and his father-in-law tortured by Union militiamen, he took to the brush and joined the even more brutal "Bloody Bill" Anderson. Along with Frank, he later took an active role in the massacre of 22 unarmed Union troops at Centralia, Missouri, and then butchered 120 others who tried to pursue the band. During the course of the war, he was wounded several times and nearly killed. And when he accidentally blew his own fingertip off in camp one day, the boyish outlaw hopped around in pain, shouting, "Ain't that the dingus dangest thing you ever saw!" From that day forward, he was known to friends as "Dingus." Only seventeen, he emerged from the war a scarred, bitter, hardened killer.

Resentful of the Reconstruction government, the brothers joined in the general anarchy in their home state, using their wartime skills to rob banks, trains and stagecoaches. They joined former guerrillas like Cole, Jim and Bob Younger and went on an unprecedented decade-long crime spree, making Missouri synonymous with banditry in the mind of much of the nation.

The year 1874 was particularly bloody. After the gang hit a stagecoach and a train, the fearsome Pinkerton Detective Agency entered the hunt. Jesse and two companions soon murdered an undercover Pinkerton agent while Jim Younger killed another in a shootout, so the agency responded by raiding the James farm on January 26, 1875. It was a fiasco. Trying to flush out the outlaws, the detectives threw either a flare or a hand grenade into the house. The device exploded, killing Jesse and Frank's thirteen-year-old half brother Archie Samuel and wounding their mother, Zerelda, so badly that her arm was amputated. The public outrage over the disaster resulted in an outpouring of sympathy for the gang and helped gain them a reputation as romantic Robin Hoods.

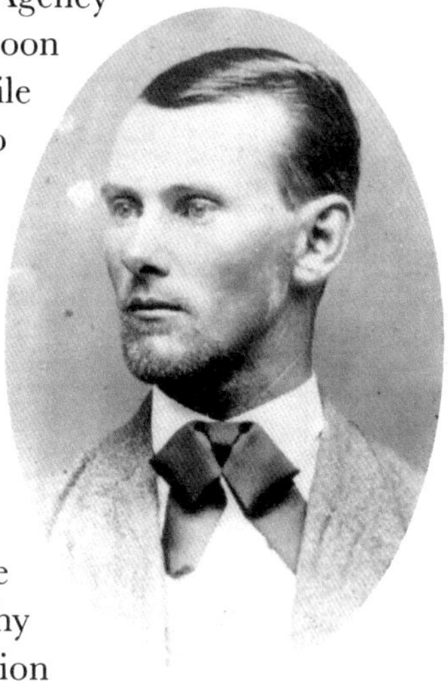

Jesse Woodson James, the legendary bandit who called Nashville home on and off for years, in a photo taken around 1875. *Library of Congress.*

The ultimate irony is that neither the James nor Younger boys seem to have been in the state at the time of the raid. With Missouri heating up, Jesse had decided to move his wife, also named Zerelda (known as Zee), to Nashville in search of a quiet hideout. In early 1875, he rented a small cottage at 606 Boscobel Street in Edgefield, which was still an independent city.

He gave his name as John Davis Howard (he preferred to be called "Dave"), and his wife went by "Josie." The Howards were a quiet couple, keeping mostly to themselves. And like most such quiet folks, they soon attracted the attention of the neighborhood window monitors. Neighbors noted how Dave Howard (who claimed to be a "wheat speculator") spent much of his time away, periodically returning flush with cash. If he was late returning home, Josie would weep and worry until he finally arrived. The neighbors soon had her sad secret figured out: they concluded their polite neighbor was really a philandering gambler, and they felt pity for his poor wife.

Jesse's domestic bliss coincided with a period of remarkable peace back home in Missouri as the gang laid low. Frank and the Younger brothers hid out in various places from Missouri to Texas. Jesse enjoyed playing the gentleman farmer in Edgefield, but he also spent at least some of his time in Chicago, stalking the hierarchy of the Pinkerton agency. He once bragged that he had William Pinkerton himself in his sights but declined to pull the trigger. "It would do me no good if I couldn't tell him about it before he died," was his reasoning.[26] However, on April 12, he made up for his self-control on that occasion. He and Frank snuck home to check on their mother, and on their way out, the brothers ambushed their neighbor Daniel Askew. Reportedly, it was he who had guided the Pinkertons the night they bombed the house. Askew died in his yard, three bullets in his head.

In the fall of 1875, Jesse and Zee abruptly moved away from their rented Edgefield cottage. Coincidentally, a bank was robbed at Huntington, West Virginia, very soon afterward. The gang was back for a new game of tag.

This one would end badly for them. On September 7, 1876, the gang attempted to take a bank at Northfield, Minnesota, but met heavy resistance. Three robbers and two citizens were killed in the shootouts that followed, and Cole, Jim and Bob Younger were captured and sent to prison. The original gang was out of business, and the James brothers decided to lie low and lick their wounds. Both Frank and Jesse returned to Tennessee in the summer of 1877.

While Jesse revived his Dave Howard persona and settled near Waverly, Frank took his brother's middle name as an alias and became "B.J. Woodson," farmer. He rented land along White's Creek near Nashville and set his hand to raising crops and trading horses. Of the two, Frank proved

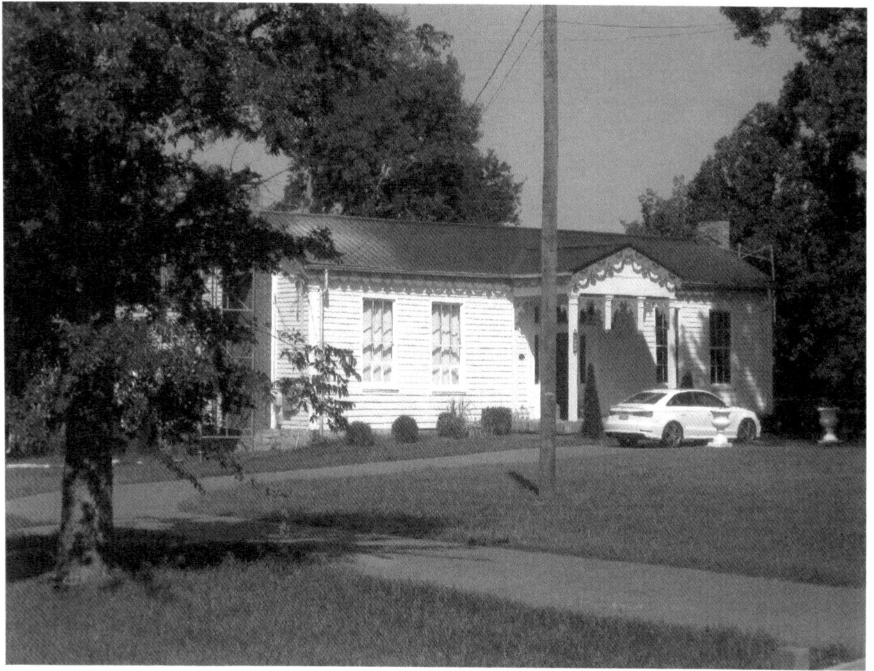

Frank James called this house on Hyde's Ferry Pike "our little home" and remembered it fondly as the only place where he enjoyed true happiness during his fugitive days. *Author's photograph.*

better at laying low; indeed, he seemed to relish his performance as a meek farmer. Formerly "accustomed to swear like a sailor,"[27] he found religion and mended his ways. He even took on the perfect disguise: that of a strong Union man from Indiana. It was effective, but it almost got him into a fight with one of his more Rebel-sympathizing neighbors. He later bragged that "I was as good a Republican as any of them."[28] Only a few times did his old instincts show themselves. On one occasion when a neighbor's son dropped by unannounced while Frank was planting corn, the outlaw turned and stuck two revolvers in the boy's face. Frank cautioned him never to approach again without announcing himself.

Meanwhile, Jesse was acting like a squirrel. He settled for a while in Humphreys County, but his tendency to flash his gun and his bad business dealings attracted too much attention. He even managed to get himself sued. Returning to Nashville in early 1879, he jumped from address to address, rarely staying put for long. He frequented the gaming tables in the "Gentleman's Quarter" and proved a lousy, if affable, gambler. Detective

Andy Rohan recalled playing Seven Up with him at Linck's Hotel near the L&N Depot on a number of occasions. He remembered the bandit as "one of the most pleasant fellows you'd want to meet....He had a soft, low voice, and...when he shook hands with you he made you think he was glad to meet you, whether he meant it or not."[29] At one point, he bought a racehorse from the Guild family of Gallatin, but he lost so heavily in a race at Atlanta that he was forced to sell the animal at a bargain price to pay his expenses home.

Worst of all, Jesse cultivated relationships with some very unstable characters. Bill Ryan (alias Tom Hill) was an Irishman with a tendency to drink and boast. Former bushwhacker Jim Cummins was later described as a "little sniveler and cry-baby."[30] They were a far cry from the Youngers, but with these misfits, it was evident that Jesse intended to form a new gang. By the spring of 1879 they were back in action, robbing a train at Glendale, Missouri.

A major rift seems to have arisen between the brothers at this point. Enjoying the security of his disguise, Frank was content to lie low and not draw new attention to himself. Jesse, on the other hand, seems to have thrived on adrenaline. The point of contention was Bill Ryan, who was a

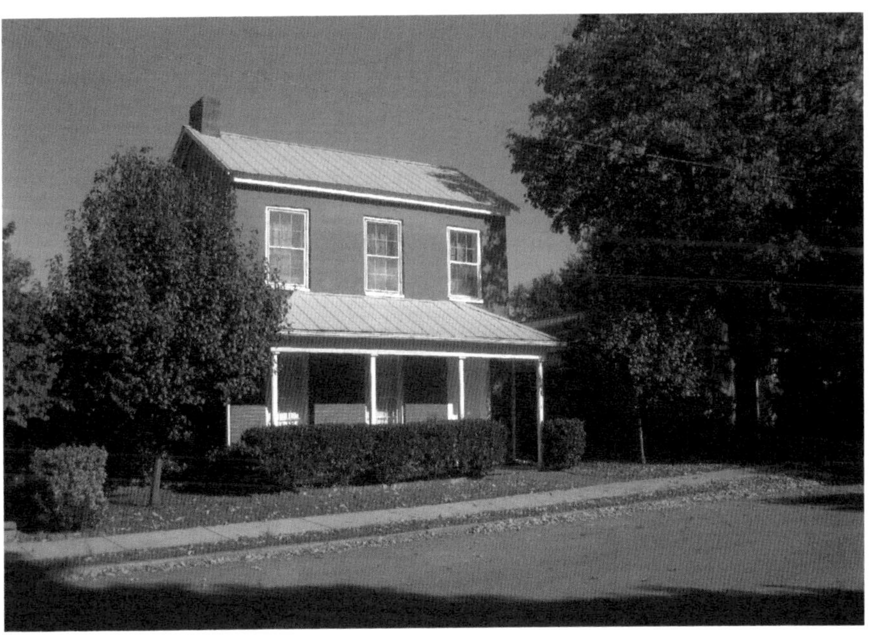

The house on Fatherland Street that Jesse rented in 1881. Bill Ryan nearly blew the back door off with a shotgun blast one night. Of all the Nashville residences Jesse lived in, this is the only one still standing. *Author's photograph.*

lightning rod for trouble. First, Ryan tried to break into the home of one of Frank's neighbors, bringing heat down on them all. When Frank passed the word to his brother "not to bring that damned Irishman to my house," a major argument broke out between the brothers, with Jesse charging that Frank just wanted to "see him dead, and see his family suffer."[31] Soon after, Ryan was at Jesse's home on Fatherland one night when the bandit was away. When he saw a suspicious figure outside, he blew the back door of the house out with a shotgun before Zee could stop him. Only some fast talk about scaring off a would-be burglar kept the authorities out of it. With drunken flakes like Ryan hanging around, disaster was just a matter of time.

The axe finally fell on March 25, 1881, as Ryan rode home after participating in a stagecoach holdup with Jesse at Muscle Shoals, Alabama. That night, he dropped into W.L. Earthman's store in White's Creek, just north of Nashville. As usual, he was soon drunk as a skunk and waving a pistol around, but unfortunately for him, Earthman was a county constable and tough as they come. With the help of some customers, he soon hogtied the hapless Ryan to a chair, then threw the chair into a wagon and drove to the county jail. Authorities found over $1,400 and two revolvers on the troublesome drunk, who was soon identified as one of the stage robbers.

The following evening, the brothers, their families and gang member Dick Liddil quietly left Nashville and the only domestic tranquility they'd known in years. "It was with despair that I drove away from our little home," Frank later recalled, "and again became a wanderer."[32]

They wandered back to Missouri, where they hit the outlaw trail again, robbing a train at Blue Cut on July 15, 1881. This robbery proved to be the swan song of the gang. Jealousy and paranoia set in, and the members began turning on one another. Several were shot dead or turned informant. Jesse began hunting down and killing associates he suspected were informing on him. Perhaps sensing his brother was on a collision course with destruction, Frank kept his distance. His instincts proved correct.

Jesse rented a small cottage at St. Joseph, Missouri, where he soon began planning to take the bank at Platte City. He brought in Bob and Charley Ford to help form a new gang, but he couldn't have picked more poorly. The Ford brothers had recently been talking to state authorities about securing pardons for themselves in exchange for the head of their boss. On April 3, 1882, while Jesse was straightening a sampler on the wall of his living room, Bob Ford leveled a .44 revolver and fired a single shot into the back of his head. "J.D. Howard" crashed awkwardly to the floor, dead at the age of thirty-five.

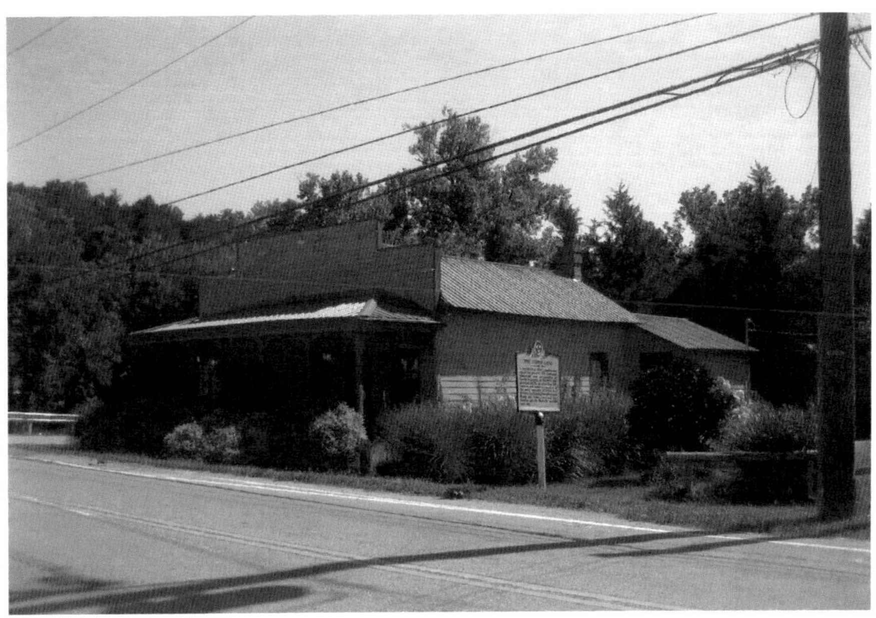

Earthman's store on White's Creek Pike, where Bill Ryan was arrested in 1881. This is the only building in Nashville with a historical marker mentioning the James gang. *Author's photograph.*

While the papers in Nashville and around the country were rife with speculation that Frank would avenge his brother's death, the older outlaw was sick of the game. He spent the next few months arranging for his surrender, and on October 5, 1882, he walked into the office of Governor Thomas T. Crittenden in Jefferson City, Missouri. Dramatically unbuckling his gun belt, he formally gave himself up. Though the governor refused to outright pardon him, his gamble paid off in the end. Following a show trial in the summer of 1883, Frank walked out of court a free man. For the first time in nearly twenty years, "Ben J. Woodson" could use his real name in public once more.

He retired to his home state, where he settled on the old family farm near Kearny, but he made frequent trips for publicity appearances—remembering, of course, to avoid Minnesota, where he was still wanted for murder. Older and wiser, he kept his nose clean and never attempted to go after his brother's killers. Even without his assistance, both came to unpleasant ends. Charley Ford committed suicide in 1884. Bob, infamous due to the folk song that branded him "the dirty little coward who shot Mr. Howard," was gunned down at Creede, Colorado, in 1892.

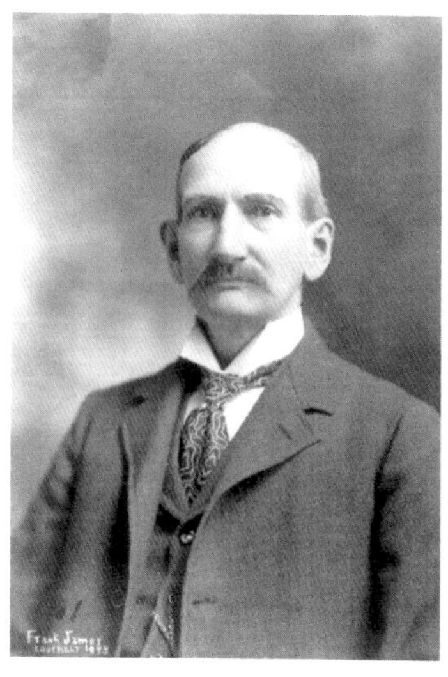

Frank James would return as a tourist to swap yarns with some of his former neighbors. This photo shows him as he looked in 1898. *Library of Congress.*

Frank took several trips back to Nashville, most notably in 1903, when he and Cole Younger came to town promoting a "Wild West" show they were producing. He was received like a visiting dignitary, touring the Civil War battlefields at Franklin and holding court for the press. His life as a fugitive had become the stuff of jokes.

For example, several Nashville policemen were fond of telling the tale of the time they got a tip that the notorious Frank James was aboard a train arriving at the Nashville station. Four cops, armed with pistols, "bounced" the train as it pulled in but found only one passenger aboard. To their surprise, it was Ben Woodson, who they all knew well, and he asked what they wanted. One of them said they had orders to intercept Frank James. Without batting an eye, "Woodson" replied, "Well, I am damn glad I ain't Frank!" They all had a good laugh about it, and the police dispersed. Only later did one recall that the whole time Frank had kept his right hand under the flap of the saddlebag over his shoulder. In hindsight, they were all probably damn glad they hadn't known he was Frank at the time.

In the end, he proved a survivor. He never really repented his outlaw years; it's more honest to say he outlived them to become a curiosity in the new age of airplanes and automobiles. He died quietly at his farm on February 18, 1915—forty-nine years and five days after the date of the James gang's first reported robbery.

When the news broke, many citizens of the city were surprised to find out their friendly neighbors had actually been wanted murderers and thieves, but in Victorian times, there were many such secrets hidden across the city. A few years after the James boys left, another such secret was laid bare. It was a whodunnit that captivated the public imagination, and it originated in the dark back streets that "respectable" people rarely talked about.

CHAPTER 4

DEATH ON BILLY GOAT HILL

Nashville has always been a surprisingly diverse town. Even during the nineteenth century, immigrants made up a significant part of the city's population, their traditions and culture adding many contributions to the fabric of the community. People of African, Irish, German, Italian, Russian, Polish, Scottish and French backgrounds put down roots here, brought by the railroad or the river, looking to make a life.

As with so many other cities, these new arrivals tended to settle into insular communities. The most prominent of these was the Ninth Ward, known as Germantown, which developed into an exclusive neighborhood after the Civil War. There you would have found newspaper publishers, brewers, merchants and other prominent citizens, mostly of German or Austrian descent, living in quiet, modest Victorian town houses.

The streets weren't paved with gold for most, though. Faced with the common fear and bigotry of the times, immigrants from other cultures were often forced to eke out an existence on the fringes of society, working in rather shady occupations and looking for opportunity wherever they could find it. Their neighborhoods tended to be rough and seedy, and most are completely forgotten today. Even longtime residents will draw a blank when asked about "Hell's Half Acre," "Slate Town," "Varmint Town" or "Crappy Chute."

Such a place was the area of Jefferson Street west of the intersection with Warren. Home to mainly poor Irish, German and African American residents, it became known for some obscure reason as "Billy Goat Hill." In

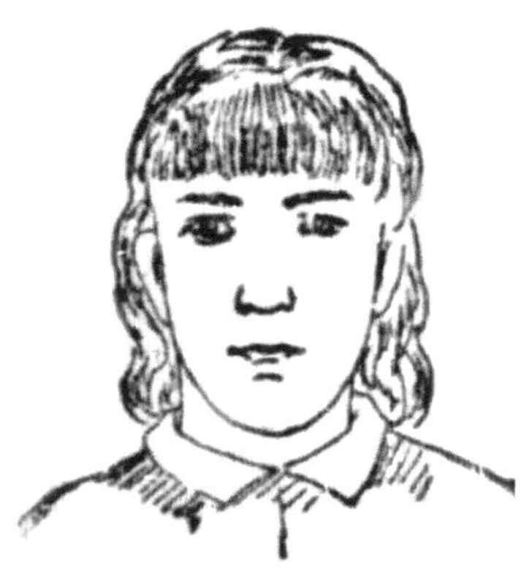

Mamie Dolan. Her only known image, from a sketch that appeared in the newspapers after her death. *Author's collection.*

its heyday, it was nothing to brag about—a teeming, violent four-block melting pot that only seemed to make the news when a "blind pig" saloon was raided or when one of the frequent fights got out of hand. When the interstate obliterated the heart of the old neighborhood in the late 1960s, nobody shed a tear.

As can be imagined, plenty of human drama had played out on these mean streets in the preceding years. And one of the strangest of these episodes began on the night of January 26, 1891, at a run-down grocery on the corner of Clay and Jefferson Streets.

It was late in the evening when Theodore Kramer, the deputy coroner of Davidson County, arrived at the scene to find a house in chaos. Doctors William P. Matthews, Percy Cleveland and Newton G. Tucker were in the process of examining the remains of a teenage girl who lay dead on a sofa in the common room, while various relatives and neighbors hovered around. Kramer immediately convened a coroner's inquest.

The deceased was fourteen-year-old Mary Ann Dolan, known as "Mamie" to her friends. Originally from Louisville, Kentucky, she was the adopted daughter of John Moran, who owned the establishment. At first glance, Mamie's body showed no obvious sign of injury other than a slight indentation and discoloration between her eyes. Her body was still warm to the touch, and rigor mortis had not set in. The doctors present estimated her time of death to be around 8:00 p.m., or approximately an hour before they arrived. That seemed to be the only fact they had to work from because none of the witnesses present could agree on any other details of her death.

Slowly, Kramer began to extract a rough picture of what had occurred. Around the time of her death, Mamie had been seated on the sofa with her closest friend, sixteen-year-old Charlotte Racknitz. At some point, she said she wished to go out onto the back porch, saying she felt sick, so Charlotte assisted her out the door. Moments later, Charlotte ran back into the house, shouting that Mamie had fallen down on the porch and wouldn't get up.

Annie Phillips, Mamie's aunt, went out and scolded her, saying, "Why don't you get up and quit making a fool of yourself?" After a while, it became apparent that something was really wrong, so Mrs. Phillips asked Mamie's boyfriend, Sam Ritter, to help pick her up. Together, they carried her into the house and laid her on the floor near the bed where Mrs. Moran was lying critically ill. As they did so, Mrs. Phillips said she noticed a small vial fall from the back of her niece's dress labeled "Poison, strychnine, one-half ounce." She died in ten minutes, according to Mrs. Phillips. The witnesses claimed that young Mamie had threatened suicide before and guessed that she'd swallowed the poison.

The bottle was half full. A quarter ounce would be approximately one hundred times more than a lethal dose for someone her age. The usual symptoms should have included muscle spasms and seizures, elevated temperature and heartbeat and *risis sardonicus*—the telltale fixed grin of strychnine poisoning. Yet the witnesses described remarkably mild symptoms for such a massive dose. "No convulsion, further than the clinching of the teeth preceded death."[33]

Something wasn't adding up, so Kramer dug deeper, and cracks began appearing in the stories. John Moran in particular was raising red flags. He had brought Mamie to Nashville a few years before after her parents died, and according to his testimony, "she had always been obedient and dutiful, and was of a merry disposition…and had been so up to the hour of her death."[34] In this, he was flatly contradicted by Sam Ritter and Charlotte Racknitz, who both testified to the bad blood that existed between Mamie and her adoptive father. Charlotte related that after Mamie had collapsed, Moran had stood over her and shouted, "Goddamn her, she ought to have been dead five years ago!" Ritter mentioned that the girl—only fourteen—had spent most of the day drinking at the saloon next door and avoiding Moran, who was himself noticeably drunk even during the inquest.

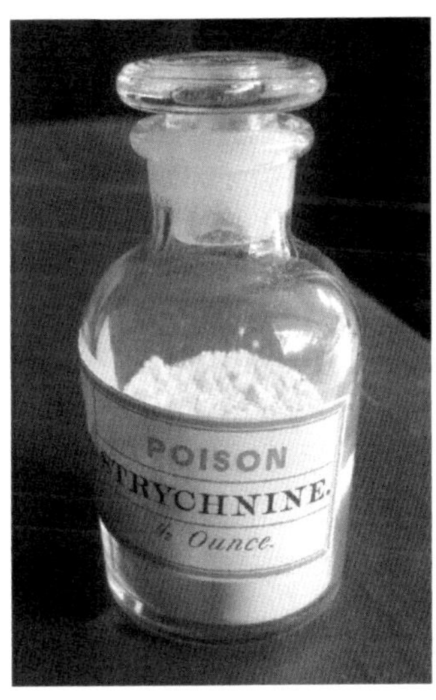

A small vial of strychnine fell from Mamie's dress after she was picked up. At the autopsy, doctors debated whether she died from poisoning. *Author's photograph.*

The proceedings were postponed until daylight, and Dr. Wharton was instructed to examine Mamie's stomach for traces of arsenic. As the second day of testimony began, a new player appeared on the scene.

John Dolan, an employee of the Louisville gas works, had been skimming the evening paper when, to his shock, he saw an account of his sister's mysterious death in Nashville. He immediately boarded a southbound train and stormed into town, raging at the Moran family for not making any attempt to notify him. He demanded to have her body turned over to him and then went to see Sheriff William J. Hill. After discussing his suspicions with officials, Dolan had warrants sworn out for the arrest of Moran and Mrs. Phillips, as well as Charlotte Racknitz; her father, Charles; and Sam Ritter. All five were hauled in and subjected to intense questioning by Detective Pat Hannifin at the jail.

Meanwhile, the doctors' suspicions were growing. They focused on the wound over Mamie's left eye, which seemed to have been made by some sort of sharp-cornered object. A small hatchet with a nail claw was found lying on a table on the porch a few feet from where Mamie fell, and when the corner of the claw was compared to the wound, it fit perfectly. Dr. Tucker also found evidence that Mamie's neck had been broken, noting that the head moved freely even after rigor mortis had set in and that the "preternatural mobility and crepitus" the doctors felt pointed to that end.[35] Charlotte Racknitz claimed Mamie's neck broke after she fell against the wall. The doctors, though, suspected that somebody had stomped on her neck after she'd fallen.

By now, public interest was at a fever pitch, and a crowd stood in a cold January rain outside the coroner's office, hoping for a sensation. They were not disappointed.

Detective Hannifin and Bennett H. Beazley, a restaurant owner and justice of the peace, appeared and announced that they had extracted a confession from young Charlotte Racknitz. In a late-night jailhouse interview, the girl had told them that Mamie had "sassed" her stepfather at supper about her going to a masquerade ball. Later, when she'd stepped out on the porch, she said a man had suddenly struck Mamie between the eyes with a hatchet and then disappeared into the darkness. Charlotte initially said she didn't recognize the man, but after some pressure, she broke down and identified the attacker as none other than "Old Man" John Moran.

Close on the heels of this bombshell came another one. Dr. Wharton appeared before the inquest and reported that two separate chemical tests had confirmed there was strychnine present in her stomach. This seemed to be incompatible with the story Miss Racknitz told, though the investigators explained it as a clumsy attempt to hide the crime. After carrying Mamie back into the house, Mrs. Phillips had administered salt water as an emetic to get her to throw up. Obviously, they surmised, the poison had been in the cup, and she had swallowed some before she died. They even theorized—though unconvincingly—that her neck had been broken during the force-feeding attempt.

With that, the coroner's jury returned their verdict: John Moran had murdered his stepdaughter with the aid of his sister-in-law, Annie Phillips. The pair were kept in jail until the evidence could be put to the grand jury, while the others were released from custody. Mamie Dolan's body was released to the care of her brother, who took her back to Louisville for burial. She was laid to rest with little ceremony a few days later at St. Louis Cemetery.

Not surprisingly, the public mood was grim. Angry crowds gathered at the jail on Front Street, hovering in an ominous fashion. Sheriff Hill was forced to double the guards and place weapons within easy reach, fearing that a mob might storm the jail. Inside, Moran sat stone-faced on his bunk, quietly speaking to friends who came to support him. He proved a tough customer. "He spoke of the weather and of politics," a reporter stated, "but seldom referred to the crime."[36]

Moran made for an attractive villain indeed. His background was murky, but he had long been a fixture in the neighborhood, and many referred to the tough old saloon man as the "King of Billy Goat Hill." He'd frequently been in the headlines for various unsavory reasons.

For instance, there was the time when he had attempted to have his brother Thomas committed at the County Insane Asylum for treatment after a spell of temporary insanity. The superintendent later recalled that he and a buddy named Henry Schisler had showed up drunk and rowdy with Thomas Moran in tow. Then, when the attendants had attempted to put him into a cell, Thomas had attacked them. During the bloody fight that ensued, John Moran had sat in a nearby office without helping in the least, while Schisler had watched the show, laughing the whole time.

A few months later, Henry Schisler himself was shot and killed by a drunken barfly after refusing to sell the man a drink. Moran had testified that he was present and had tried to placate the assailant, but once again, he'd been in the next room when the shooting happened and had not intervened.

The image of John Moran that emerged was that of a hard-bitten man, habitually drunk and abusive, who attacked everything close to him. Even his wife, Bridget, who lay dying of cancer at that very moment, was often subjected to his alcoholic rage. On the very night Mamie died, he had reportedly been "raising sand" with everybody in the house and had gotten so abusive toward Bridget that the other women sitting in the room with him had forced him to leave. All in all, it was the picture of a perfect suspect—a man fully capable of killing on the slightest pretext in a drunken "brown out" without remembering a thing afterward.

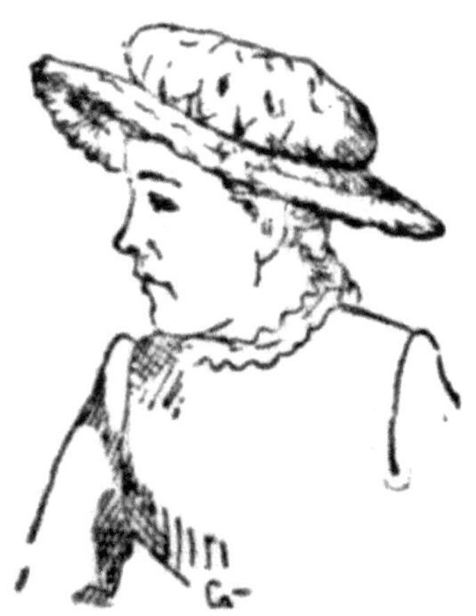

Lottie Racknitz, from a sketch made by a newspaper artist while she testified. Her testimony ended in one of the most dramatic moments ever seen in a Davidson County courtroom. *Author's collection.*

However, when it came to a motive, the investigators hit a wall. A rumor went around that Moran's dying wife had willed everything to the victim and that he had killed the girl to keep her from inheriting a fortune. It was nonsense. Moran and his wife owned their property jointly, and any such will would have required his consent and signature. An even more dreadful motive was ruled out when the doctors testified that their examination had "emphatically contradicted" any possibility of sexual assault.[37] They were left with the assumption that he had killed the girl simply because he was drunk and mean when he did it—which was certainly within the realm of possibility.

The case was complicated by the fact that many of the principals were related, and all seemed unwilling to tell everything they knew. When Moran was confronted in jail with the confession of Lottie Racknitz, he said it was "all wrong....I thought too much of that child to harm her." Then he added a cryptic postscript about his sister-in-law and codefendant. "Mrs. Phillips could tell more about this affair than I can," he said. "Mrs. Phillips can tell you."[38] He then drifted into silence and refused to speak further. Annie Phillips was more chatty but proved adept at dodging the difficult questions and shed no light on Moran's accusation. The details of her story kept shifting suspiciously. In the end, the grand jury indicted both of them for first-degree murder, and they began the long wait for their trial date.

In the meantime, the family was hit by an additional tragedy. On April 6, Bridget Moran passed away at the couple's home on Jefferson Street. She was forty years old and had been bedridden for over a year. There is no record of how Moran took the news in his jail cell.

It would take seven months and much legal maneuvering before the case finally came to trial. On the morning of September 22, 1891, court was called to order, and the players took their positions. John Moran was deadly serious after his months of enforced sobriety. The courts noted how "imperturbable and unreadable" his face was.[39] He took a seat next to his formidable defense team, headed up by General Andrew Jackson Caldwell, a former congressman and district attorney.

Before the proceedings even began, the first sensational moment came when the attorney general, Laps D. McCord, moved to have charges against Mrs. Annie Phillips dismissed, admitting that he didn't feel the evidence was strong enough against her for a conviction. Relieved, she soon took her leave of the courtroom.

After some difficulty, a jury was impaneled, and the testimony began. The state started off by introducing medical witnesses to give their opinions about the cause of death, but the real show would take place the following day, as star witness Lottie Racknitz was to take the stand and accuse John Moran of murder. The promise of drama saw the courtroom packed to capacity at nine o'clock the next morning as the judge's gavel fell. But the drama that followed exceeded most of their wildest expectations.

Dr. W.D. Matthews was up first to finish the medical testimony, and when he stepped down, the prosecution team asked the bailiff to "Call Charlotte Racknitz." Every head turned to follow her as she settled into the witness seat.

She proved a most timid witness, avoiding eye contact and answering in a quiet, hesitant manner. Several times the judge had to ask her to speak up. She repeated her original story, swearing that Moran had struck Mamie with the hatchet before rushing off into the darkness. She said she thought he'd run around the house unseen and then joined the family unnoticed when they came out on the porch to tend to the fallen Mamie. Drunk and angry, he'd picked up his adopted daughter's body and shook it like a rag doll, damning her and saying that "she ought to have been dead five years ago." It was heady stuff.[40]

But when General Caldwell began to cross-examine her, things started coming off the rails. Gently, he began questioning her. She was confronted with a story she'd earlier told reporters, in which Lottie claimed that Mamie had shown her a bottle of strychnine the very morning she died, saying that she was depressed. Mamie said that she feared her ailing "Aunt Bridget" was about to die, and if so, she'd be sent home to Louisville, a place she evidently dreaded. She said she would kill herself before that happened. At first, Lottie tried to deny this had occurred, but under further questioning, she admitted it was true.

From this point forward, her testimony degenerated into a series of "yes, sir" and "no, sir" as she was walked back through the story. She seemed confused and upset. And then came a decisive moment:

Q. Didn't Mamie say she was sick and wanted to throw up?

A. Yes, sir.

Q. Is not that what she went out for?

A. Yes, sir.

Q. Didn't she simply fall down and fall violently on her face?

A. Yes, sir.

Q. Now, did anybody hit her?

A. No, sir, I will tell the truth.[41]

There was a murmur and a burst of applause that quickly died. Dead silence reigned in the courtroom for several seconds. The defense team began grinning. The prosecution looked stunned.

On further questioning from both sides, Lottie Racknitz claimed that Detective Hannifin and Justice Beazley had coerced a confession out of her by threatening to hang her father for the crime if she didn't pin it on Moran—a charge that drew harsh denials from both men. When the prosecution tried to question her as to who had gotten her to change her story, General Caldwell pounced with proper Victorian gallantry. He objected that legally she could not be so questioned, roaring, "For the sake of this poor child, if the Court please, I want the rule insisted upon. She has had trouble enough!"[42] Charlotte Racknitz was dismissed and stepped down from the dock.

Mustering what tattered dignity he could, Attorney General McCord stood and addressed the court. "I fully believe the girl was murdered, but I am unable to prove it," he said. "Therefore, I ask that the jury be instructed to bring in a verdict of 'not guilty.'"[43] Moran was duly discharged and walked out a free man that day, his many friends pounding his back in congratulation. Hollywood couldn't have scripted it better.

After this jaw-dropping finale, the major players slipped quietly back into their lives, leaving many unanswered questions behind. Moran was never brought back to court, nor was anyone else ever charged with Mamie's murder. Why did the state drop its case so quickly and thoroughly? Was there truth to the allegation that Beazley and Hannifin had tampered with witness testimony? Both men released formal statements to the press vehemently denying the charges, and neither of them was ever disciplined or removed from duty. In company with the witnesses in the case, the attorney general left a distinct impression that he wasn't telling the whole story behind his sudden and humiliating retreat.

And there's the biggest question of all: was Mary Ann Dolan really murdered? If so, who did it and why?

There are major problems with the medical evidence presented. The initial examination settled on the hatchet as the murder weapon, saying there were no protrusions or projections on the porch floor that might have caused Mamie's injuries. Yet one witness pointed to a protruding shutter hinge she might have struck as she fell. As far as the obvious injuries to her neck area, they were never explained.

Was it suicide? She obviously had access to strychnine, as the vial found on her body had been in the Moran house for months. She also had motivation, given her beloved aunt's pending death and her own dreaded return to Kentucky. Certainly, suicide is plausible, but if she swallowed poison, then where did the additional injuries come from? It's unlikely she could have broken her own neck.

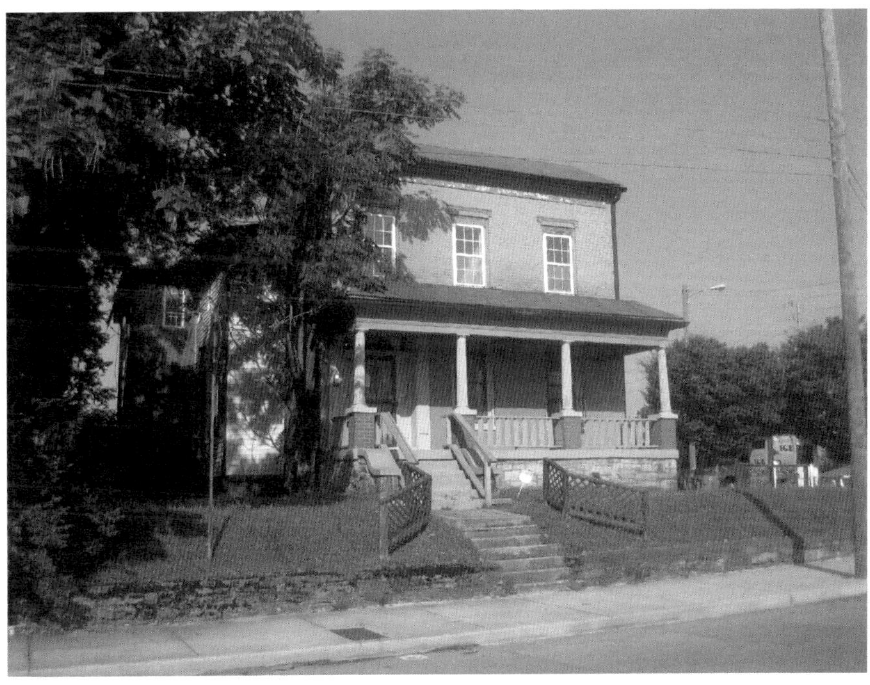

Lone survivor. This small house, built in 1900, is one of the last remaining structures from a time when this neighborhood was infamous as Billy Goat Hill. *Author's photograph.*

Were the authorities missing the real killer? A fascinating statement came from Charles Racknitz, Lottie's father, who told a friend, "If anyone killed her, it must have been either my little girl, Moran or Ritter."[44] It seems an odd thing for a father to say. Of the three, Moran was acquitted, and Sam Ritter was sitting in front of witnesses at the moment Mamie died. Charlotte, on the other hand, was alone with Mamie when she died and had ample time and opportunity. Her story also kept changing in a suspicious manner. But what motivation did she have? Could she really have harbored a grudge so deep she decided to kill one of her best friends and afterward give no indication of it? It seems hard to believe.

Or was it an accident? Sam Ritter testified that Mamie had spent the afternoon drinking because of the tension in the house. Shocking as it seems, in that era one only needed to be tall enough to see over the bar to purchase a drink. Did she die of acute alcohol poisoning? And if so, why didn't the doctors find any sign of it in her autopsy?

Mamie Dolan is beyond those concerns. Like Billy Goat Hill itself, she lies forgotten today among the shadows of the Victorian monuments that tower above her grave. Her mysterious end is still unresolved and probably always will be.

In fiction, the detectives always neatly tie up all the loose ends, but in real life, it doesn't work that way. Some mysteries linger for decades, haunting the people of the community with unanswered questions. Our next chapter will amply illustrate that.

CHAPTER 5

SLAUGHTER IN PARADISE

The evening of March 23, 1897, was a typically quiet spring night for the farming families living along what was then called Paradise Ridge. Fifteen miles northwest and a world apart from the bright lights of downtown Nashville, the Ridge was sparsely populated and isolated. Folks here rose and set with the sun, and when darkness descended, it was impenetrable. Most people didn't stray far from their hearthsides after dark.

E. Henry Simpson was sitting up that night with a sick friend. About ten o'clock, he stepped into the backyard to draw water from the well and noticed something that shocked him to his core: a bright flickering light half a mile to the east, illuminating the surrounding forest. Quickly, he saddled his horse and rode through the darkness to the scene of the fire.

It was the home of the Ade family, his nearest neighbors. By the time he arrived, the house was hopelessly engulfed. He called out, asking if anyone was there. There was no answer.

Wanting to do something, he broke in the door of the nearby smokehouse and began pulling out the meat hanging within, trying to save something from the wreckage. As he did so, embers set that structure alight and the heat forced him to abandon the effort. About that time, the Ades' toothless old shepherd dog approached from out of the gloom, limping and seemingly injured. Uncharacteristically, the tough old hound hovered close to Simpson, whimpering and seeking comfort. Backlit by the flickering flames against the silent woods, Simpson began to get a spooky feeling.

The walls of the burning house finally collapsed in a shower of sparks, and the fire began to die down. That's when he caught sight of what looked like bundles of rags lying in the embers near the still-standing chimney. Simpson found a potato fork nearby and tied it to a long pole. Reaching into the fire, he stuck the fork into one of the bundles and immediately retched. The sickly smell of burning flesh wafted through the air accompanied by an audible sizzling that sounded like a steak cooking. It was then that he realized this was going to be much worse than just a fire in the night.

Daylight revealed the extent of the horror. The neighbors managed to pick through the ashes and recover the bodies of the entire family: Jacob Ade, age fifty-seven, and his wife, Pauline, fifty, along with their eighteen-year-old daughter Lizzie and thirteen-year-old son Henry. Rosa Morier, the ten-year-old daughter of a neighbor, had been visiting the family, and her body was also recovered, along with the family's other dog. Sheriff John D. Sharp was called, and his suspicions were immediately raised by what he found.

The family's bodies were charred beyond recognition, the heads and limbs burned away. All were found in one room, which doubled as both the sitting room and the Ades' bedroom. The dog had been locked in a storage room when the fire had engulfed the house. The poor animal had backed into the fireplace, where it was finally overcome and killed.

As for the humans, there were indications that they were most likely dead already when the fire got to them. The room in which they were found had four exits to it, and it beggared belief that the fire could have overwhelmed them so quickly that none escaped.

There were also suspicious marks found on the remains. All the bodies were decapitated, but whether it was done with a blade or as a result of the fire was hard to say. Little Rosa's body was less fire-damaged than the others, and her left arm was frozen defensively above her head, the hand missing at the wrist. The back of her skull was also crushed. It appeared that the family had been murdered before the fire, possibly with an axe or with a sledgehammer found in the ruins.

As far as the authorities could tell, the murderer entered the room while the family members were chatting with one another. Apparently, Jacob was killed first, then young Henry. It seemed that the women rushed to the one window in the room and managed to get a shutter open before the killer—or killers—turned on them as well, slaughtering them where they stood. Possibly an accomplice outside had pushed them back into the window as they tried to flee. Then it seemed that bodies were decapitated and the house

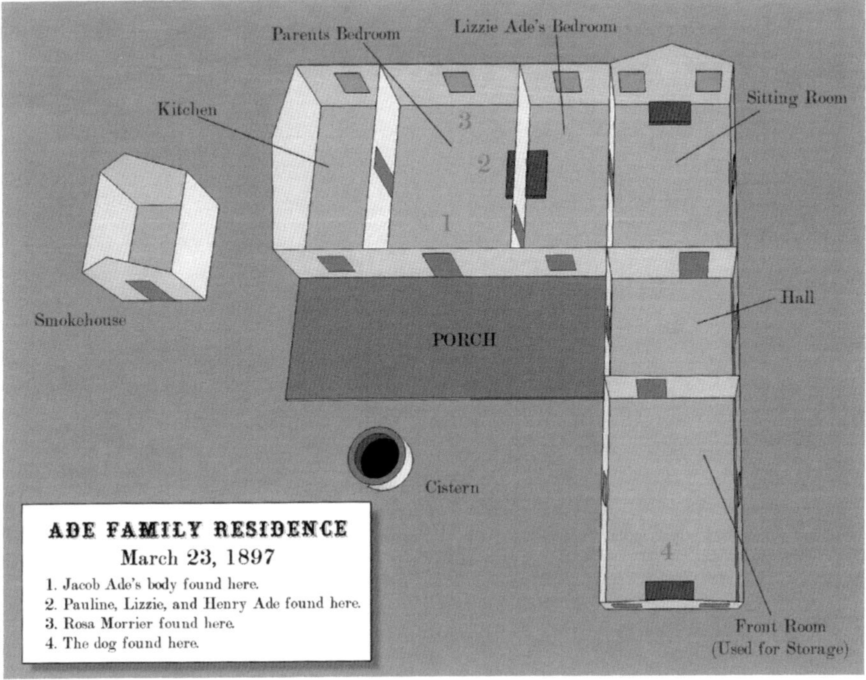

A reconstruction of the Ade family home, showing where the bodies were recovered after the fire. All the victims were found in one room. *Author's diagram.*

fired before the perpetrators fled. A neighbor spoke to the family at 7:30 p.m. and the flames were first noticed around 9:00 p.m., fixing the time of death somewhere in between. Whoever did it seemed to slip in like a ghost before vanishing without a trace.

Paradise Ridge was no stranger to violence, of course. Killings for personal reasons or over the lucrative moonshine business were not unheard of, but the wholesale slaughter of a family was unprecedented, and the neighbors were stunned—most particularly because the target of the attack was such an unlikely victim.

Jacob Ade was born in Prussia and moved to Tennessee from West Virginia sometime around 1870. He purchased the home he lived in from the Garrett family around 1875 and settled in as one of the most quiet and respected members of the community. Little description of the family survives beyond the fact that Jacob spoke with a thick German accent and the recollection that Lizzie was "a very fleshy girl."[45] Despite his rather modest dwelling, Jacob was one of the wealthiest men on the Ridge, with a 410-acre farm and stocks and bonds valued at several thousand dollars. He was known as a moneylender who often floated loans to his neighbors when needed. Just the day before he died, he had been in Nashville, where he had deposited $2,000 at Fourth National Bank and had withdrawn $200, which he loaned to his neighbor Tom Williams.

However, if robbery was the object, the attackers had missed their mark. The neighbors were quite well informed and knew that Ade kept little money in the house. In fact, a charred tomato can was located in the ruins with the burnt remains of what cash there was—a grand total of $19.55. The killers hadn't even taken this small sum.

So if robbery wasn't the motive, could it be revenge? The sheriff questioned the neighbors and surviving Ade family members, and they all said the same thing: you need to talk to Ed Anderson.

If Ade had an enemy, it was Anderson, who bore an unsavory reputation on the Ridge. He lived a mile from the scene, and at one time he had been friends with Ade. In fact, one of the family's two dogs had originally been a gift from him. However, things had soured to the point that Ade swore out a warrant against his neighbor for stealing three of his hogs. Anderson was arrested for the theft on the Saturday before the massacre.

Despite this promising lead, the investigation stalled. Anderson came in voluntarily for questioning but was let go, as there was no real evidence against him. Despite a $1,150 reward, no viable tips came in, and the trail went cold. A hasty inquest was held on a plank in the front yard, which came

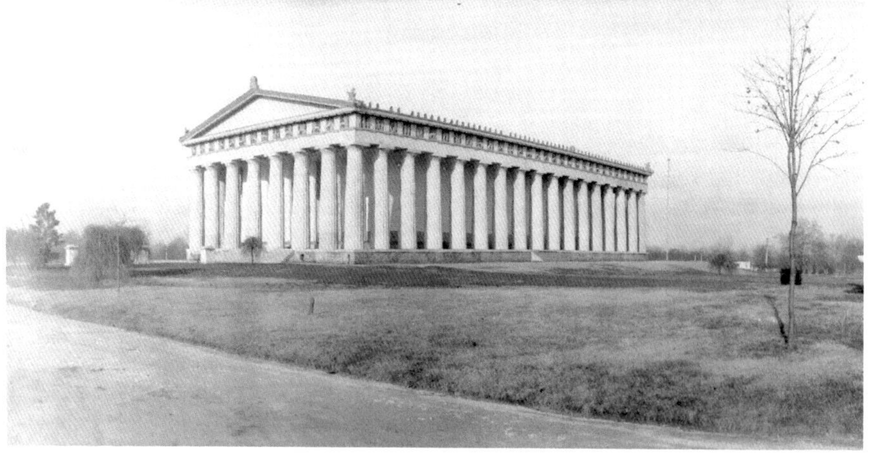

The Parthenon, centerpiece of the Tennessee Centennial Exposition, which opened a short time after the Ade murders. Some speculated the killer might have come to town to work on the exhibition. *Library of Congress.*

to an obvious conclusion: the victims were murdered by a person or persons unknown. Afterward, the pitiful remains were gathered together. There was so little left that the bones of the entire Ade family were placed in one coffin, while those of Rosa Morier were placed into another. They were all buried near the shell of the burned-out house. And that's where things rested for over half a year.

Then suddenly, the case broke wide open. Sheriff Sharp's bulldog, Deputy Sam Borsum, went to work with a vengeance, and that October he staged a series of raids, quickly rounding up five suspects. There were two African American men, Lee Hunter and Jim Elliott. Prime suspect Ed Anderson was taken in, along with his brother Dave. And most shocking of all was the arrest of Henry Morier. The father of little Rosa who died in the slaughter was now accused of killing his own daughter and throwing her body into the burning house.

Lee Hunter was the state's chief witness, and he claimed that the white men had killed the family as revenge for them prosecuting Anderson on the hog theft charge. Little Rosa, he claimed, had recognized her father and begged for her life. He said Mr. Morier had growled, "Dead men tell no tales," before bashing her head in and throwing her into the burning house. Hunter said he was paid forty dollars to set fire to the place and that he'd been caught in a back draft and burned his hand while doing so. He had the scars to back up his claim.

However, there were immediate problems with the case. Rumor got around that Borsum had gotten a couple of informants to coax drunken confessions out of Hunter and Elliott. And the doctor who treated Hunter the day after the fire said that his injury wasn't a burn but a dog bite.

In the summer of 1898, as the war with Spain dominated the headlines, the five men had their day in court. Despite the long hours in the saddle by Deputy Borsum, the evidence was ultimately not convincing. Hunter was a shiftless ne'er-do-well, and it became clear he would say anything to save his own neck. In addition, his story just didn't make sense. After all, why would the killers risk bringing so many people into the plot? And was it plausible that they would cold-bloodedly kill five people only to suddenly lose their nerve and pay two other men to set fire to the house and bodies? The evidence against Morier was particularly weak and seemed to stem from Elliott's testimony, as well as the fact that he had once threatened to kill Deputy Borsum over a personal grievance. The first trial ended with the charges against Elliott and Dave Anderson dismissed and a hung jury for the other three. A second trial was held, but on October 12, 1898, Ed Anderson,

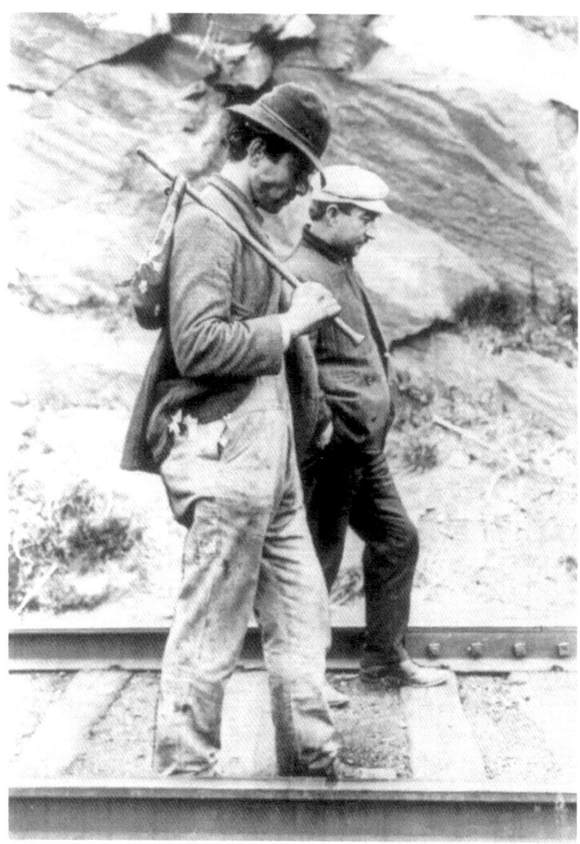

Hoboes walking the rails. Many transients were ejected from Nashville before the Centennial opened, leading some to speculate that one of them may have committed the murders. *Library of Congress.*

Morier and Hunter were all acquitted. The authorities were back to square one, their lead suspect completely exonerated. For two more years, the case lay dormant.

In June 1900, the murders came back into the public eye as two inmates at the Tennessee State Prison, Thomas O'Brien and George Newland, were formally charged with the slayings. The two were pretty unsympathetic characters who had run a successful cattle-rustling ring in Cheatham County until they were caught and convicted in February 1899. O'Brien had been a blacksmith whose shop was near the Ade place, and he was overheard telling Newland before the killing that Old Man Ade had plenty of money in the house and that he'd seen it. The pair was indicted, their trial scheduled for November 1901.

It was a strange affair from the beginning. The state's leading witnesses were the brothers and sisters of the accused. Mrs. Bettie Hancock, for example, was George Newland's sister. What's more, she had also once been O'Brien's live-in girlfriend, and she had plenty to say. The killings, she testified, came just a few days after her brother George was married. On the night of the murders, the two had packed some provisions before heading into the woods together. The day afterward, she saw them sitting together on the back porch, their faces and hair "smutty" with some kind of dark substance. A neighbor confirmed that he'd seen the two of them the afternoon of the murder just eight miles from the Ade place, heading in that general direction.

The defense came back with allegations that the witnesses in the case had planned to split the reward money three ways if Newland and O'Brien were convicted. They also put forward their theory that the murder was no murder at all—a lightning strike, they posited, could have killed everyone in the room at once and set the house on fire. This despite the fact that only one of the many witnesses called remembered a lightning storm that evening. Most said the night was clear. The state responded with the evidence of violence on the bodies, pointing out that "lightening [*sic*] does not brain dogs and people."[46]

The evidence was stronger this time, but the result was still a disappointment. In the end, the jury came back locked at eleven to one for conviction. The prisoners were confined to their cells in the jail pending a retrial.

George Newland wouldn't live to see it. Seriously ill with consumption, he rapidly declined in the damp and squalid conditions of his cell. On the evening of May 10, 1902, he bid farewell to his cellmate, asking him to "meet him in heaven" before lapsing into a coma.[47] He died hours later at the age of twenty-five. He left behind his former wife and a three-year-old daughter.

Tom O'Brien would be put on trial twice more, and the state made an all-out effort to hang him. There was new evidence this time, such as the story of merchant John Brinkley, who claimed that O'Brien was in his place with a good deal of cash shortly after the crime. When he asked where the money had come from, O'Brien asked him if he'd heard of the Ade murders. Brinkley allowed that he had. "Well," O'Brien cryptically replied, "you know old Tom."[48]

In the end, though, it was all just hearsay. On March 9, 1903, Tom O'Brien was found not guilty and walked forth a free man. And as he went, he carried with him the last chance of justice ever being done in the case. Aside from a rather sordid lawsuit between the surviving Ade children and a neighbor whom they claimed defrauded them over their father's estate, the affair finally faded from the public mind.

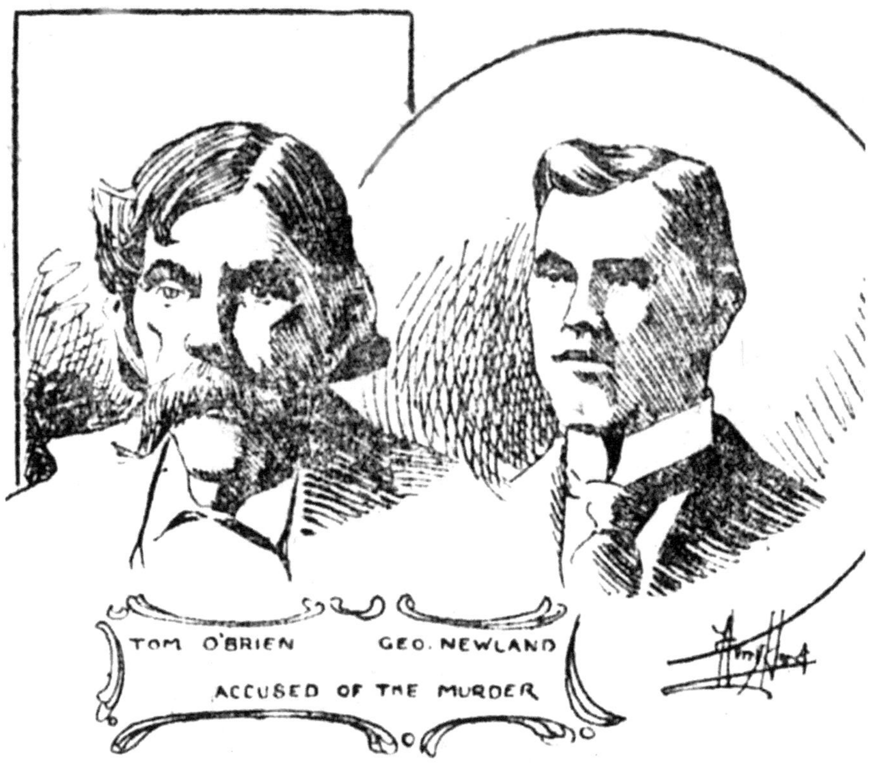

Tom O'Brien and George Newland, from a sketch made while they were on trial for the Paradise Ridge murders. *Courtesy Tennessee State Library and Archives.*

For over a century, the question of who killed the Ade family and why has remained unanswered. Some believe that the right suspects were tried but freed for lack of proof. But the evidence against the Andersons, O'Brien and Newland was nothing but hearsay from unreliable witnesses who all had their own agendas.

Others were suspected of the crime. After his acquittal, Henry Morier went on to accuse Henry Simpson, the neighbor who was first on the scene, of starting the fire. The accusation was not convincing. Bitter from the loss of his daughter and his legal troubles, Morier appears to have lashed out in anger at nearly everyone. Considering that Simpson's only prior record involved "disturbing public worship and using profane language," it seems a bit of a stretch to accuse him of mass murder.[49]

Or perhaps there was another suspect who went undetected. At the time, some suspected a hobo or tramp of killing the family, which ties in neatly with a more recent theory that an undiscovered serial killer was to blame. This theory claims that a phantom killer rode the rails in those days, striking at random and slaughtering his victims before moving on in places as far apart as Villisca, Iowa, and Columbia, Missouri. Some have tried to tie the Paradise Ridge tragedy to this pattern.

The problems are many, though. If such a killer did exist, his crimes seem to be concentrated in a period from 1911 to 1913—fourteen years after the Tennessee killings. He worked hundreds of miles away in the Midwest, and the modus operandi was much different. The weapons don't even seem to match up. While many refer to the Ade case as an "axe murder," the most likely weapon was the sledgehammer found in the ruins. Finally, even though the Nashville police were busily chasing hoboes out of town in preparation for the upcoming Centennial exposition, there have never been railroad tracks anywhere close to Paradise Ridge. It seems unlikely a stranger could avoid notice in such a tightknit community in the days after the crime.

A lot has changed in the century and a quarter since the murders. Paradise Ridge is still rural but far more connected to the world than it was then.

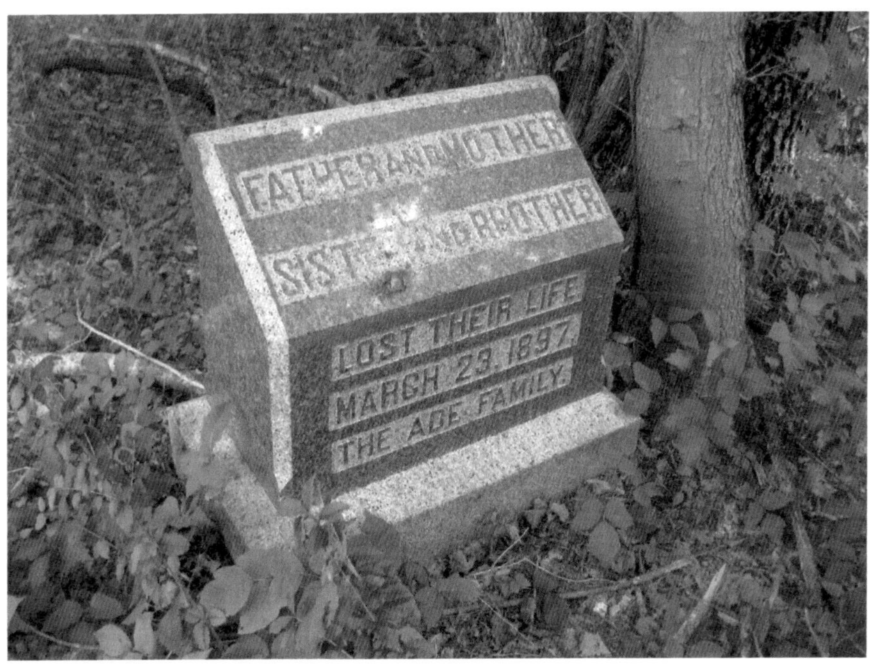

This small stone marks the former site of the family home. The remains of the Ade family and little Rosa Morier lie buried here. *Author's photograph.*

Crimes like this, once so unthinkable, have become more commonplace, and the memory of the tragedy has faded with time. There are no reminders left anymore—that is, except one.

In a quiet patch of trees sits a small stone. Nobody seems to remember exactly when it was placed there. Along the top is a simple inscription: "Father and Mother, Sister and Brother, Lost Their Life, March 23, 1897… THE ADE FAMILY." Nearby, in unmarked graves, lie the five victims, bound together in death as in life.

One hopes they rest in peace.

CHAPTER 6

ANNIE AND HARVEY

It's safe to say she turned heads.

Tall and stately, dressed in an expensive black suit with a huge picture hat resting on a crown of dark auburn hair, she walked into the lobby of the Fourth National Bank on Third Avenue at a quarter to three on October 14, 1901, just fifteen minutes before the bank closed for the day.

She walked primly up to the teller's window and flashed a charming smile, a couple of gold teeth glittering as she did so. She asked to have some money changed. Not an unusual transaction, to be sure, but the amount must have taken teller Spencer McHenry aback. Placing $550 on the marble counter, mostly in $10 notes "which had never been folded," she asked that they be changed for hundreds and fifties.

Nor was the amount the only odd part of her request. The ten-spots were not normal legal tender notes. Instead, they were national currency bills issued to the Bank of Montana at Helena. And something about them set off alarm bells in McHenry's mind.

Thinking quickly, he asked the lovely lady to have a seat; after all, these sorts of transactions took a bit of time. He then stepped into the back office and conferred with cashier Joseph Howell, and the two concurred—the bills matched a bulletin describing the loot from the train robbery at Wagner, Montana, back in July. While Howell stalled the woman, McHenry phoned the central police station.

Minutes later, Detectives Austin H. Dickens and Jack Dwyer walked in and placed the woman under arrest, escorting her down to headquarters.

Nobody realized it at the time, but this seemingly unremarkable incident marked the first step in the final downfall of one of the most famous gangs of the Old West.

On July 3, 1901, three gunmen had stopped the Union Pacific's Great Northern Flyer at Wagner, Montana. They shot three people, dynamited the safe and made off with nearly $40,000 in uncirculated bills. The robbery was headline news, and authorities had been on the lookout for the loot for months. A few bills had surfaced in Baltimore and Chicago that had obviously been professionally laundered. "The work of this woman was very amateurish," opined Edward S. Gaylor, head of the Pinkerton Detective Agency's Chicago office. She obviously didn't know enough to weather the bills to make them look old before cashing them. "I do not think she is alone here," he added.[50]

After her arrest, Annie Rogers had her mug shot taken by society photographer Carl Giers, who was charmed by his subject. This previously unpublished image ran in the local press. *Author's collection.*

The police knew they'd made a major collar, but who was this mystery woman? It's a question that still hasn't been fully answered to this day. She gave her name at various times as Annie Rogers and Maude Williams, but as to where she came from or where she was staying in Nashville, she refused to answer. She simply said she had the money legally and protested that she'd done nothing to warrant such treatment. The detectives fanned out through town, trying to locate her hotel room on the assumption she had more of the stolen loot stashed in her trunk.

Annie proved as captivating to her jailers as they were to her, particularly the gruff Detective Dwyer, whom Annie flirted with incessantly. He seemed to melt when she laughingly referred to him as "Happy Jack." The press was fascinated, describing her "piercing black eyes...that fairly dance as she speaks."[51] Many tried to downplay her looks, but it is apparent that most agreed with the reporter who wrote that she was "a rather good looking young woman" with "the bearing of a coquettish girl."[52] She flashed two gold teeth when she laughed, which she did a great deal. They tried to draw her out in interviews, but Annie proved to be no fool and expertly danced around their questions. All they could get out of her was that she claimed to be twenty-six, and based on her accent and manner of speaking, she was of limited education and grew up in Texas.

Even now, with the hindsight of more than a century, it's hard to make heads or tails of Annie's life. She told a plausible story, but she was truthful only as often as it suited her, and thus far, records that might confirm her tale have remained elusive. She claimed she was born in Tarrant County, Texas, and that she ran away from home around 1893 when she was eighteen—the implication being that she went to work in a brothel, either in Texas or Arkansas. Around three years later, she said she married a farmer named Lewis Walker. She later left him—quite frankly because she was bored. Around 1900, she went to work in Fanny Porter's high-class bordello in San Antonio, and that's where she first comes into the public record.

In the fall of that year, going by "Maud Walker," she attended the International Fair in company with a co-worker named Lillie Davis. The pair hooked up with two well-heeled gentlemen calling themselves "Bob Nevilles" and "William Casey." Their real names were Harvey Logan and Will Carver, and they were two of the main members of the notorious outlaw gang known as the Wild Bunch.

Logan, who was better known as "Kid Curry," was an interesting paradox. Outwardly quiet, of short stature, with a mild, sad-looking face, he was at heart a cunning criminal and a born killer. He was a deadly gunman with a hunter's patience. Rumor has it that even while he was fleeing the Wagner train holdup with posses hot on his trail, he took the time to ambush and kill an old enemy before leaving Montana. This was one of at least six murders he was suspected of having a hand in.

After that, he picked up Annie, and the pair began a whirlwind tour of the South from Shreveport to Memphis, shopping in the best stores and laundering the money through underworld contacts in brothels and saloons. They were on the road for about a month before they came to Nashville and registered at Linck's Hotel near the railroad depot on October 10. Incredibly, they registered using his real name as Mr. and Mrs. Logan.

The morning of her arrest, she told Harvey she was going shopping. In reality, she had squirreled away $500 of the loot without Logan's knowledge to use as a nest egg. In fact, it appears that she went to the bank instead of using one of their underworld contacts so that Logan wouldn't find out about it. When she didn't return that evening, he didn't waste time asking questions. As Annie stalled her interrogators down at the station house, Logan grabbed everything and left town that night. By the time the police traced him days later, he was long gone.

Annie was reasonably honest about her background and where the money came from, though the short, dark Logan became a little blond man named "Charley" in her version. She claimed "Charley" left her at Shreveport for New Orleans and she'd gone on alone to Nashville.[53] She let slip that she was quite experienced at "the game," stating at one point that she often picked up such men and "that she would rather play the road and hotels than stay in a regular bawdy house."[54]

Her cool demeanor began to break down as the officers transferred her from holding to county jail. At her arraignment, when asked how she pled to the charges against her, Annie's Texas temper flared. "Guilty of what?" she snapped. "Of taking those bills to the bank?...Yes, I did that!" In the end, she pleaded not guilty and was unable to make the whopping $10,000 bond, saying, "I know nobody here."[55] As she was remanded to jail, she broke down crying, but if the officers were hoping she was about to crack, they were mistaken. She quickly composed herself and headed back to jail without a word. Until a proper cell was ready, she was confined to the hospital ward.

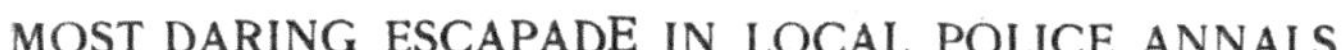

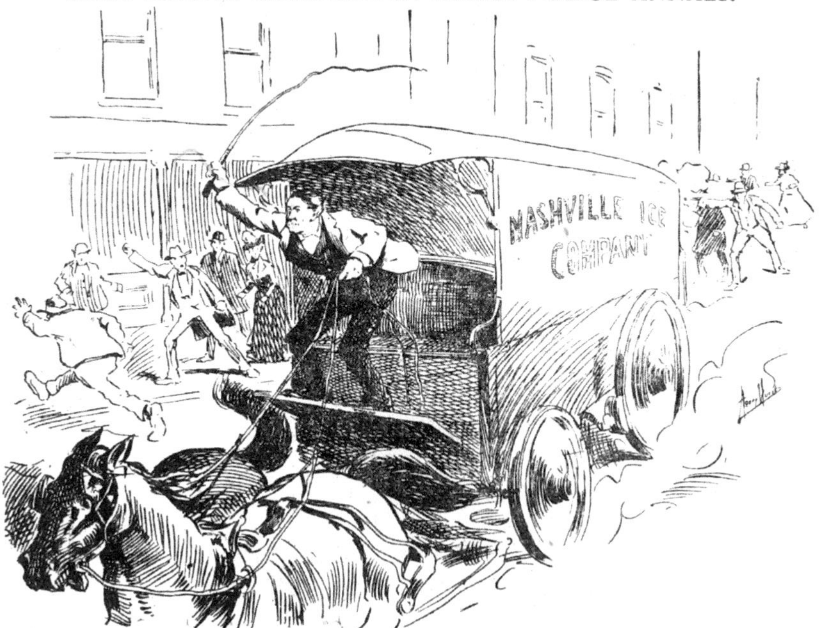

Bandit stands off two detectives and escapes in an ice wagon.

Train robber O.C. Hanks shot his way out of town in an incident remembered as the "Ice Wagon Chase," due to the unorthodox vehicle he commandeered. *Author's collection.*

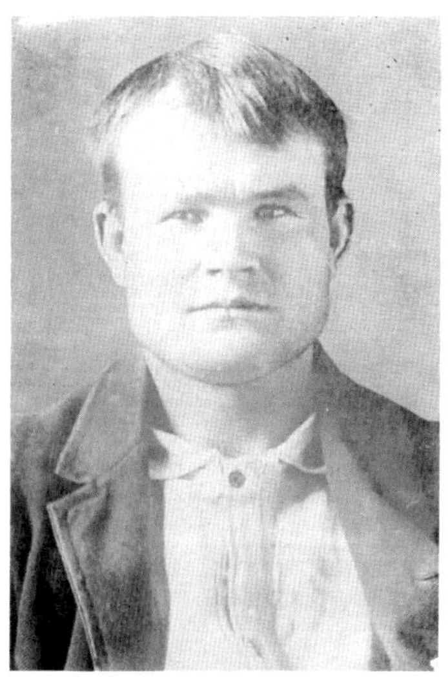

For some time, the local press speculated that the ice wagon man was none other than Butch Cassidy himself, seen here. However, at the time of the events in Nashville, Cassidy and the Sundance Kid had already fled to South America. *Library of Congress.*

Meanwhile, the plot thickened. On October 27, a rough-looking man tried to pass another of the Montana bills at Newman's clothing store on North College Street. Detectives Dwyer and Dickens once more went to arrest him, but their suspect fought back viciously, pulled a six-shooter and hijacked a passing ice wagon. In this unlikely getaway vehicle, he crossed the Woodland Street Bridge in a hail of gunfire. The chase lasted several miles before the man shook his pursuers and escaped into the Shelby Bottoms. Nobody was hit, but the detectives had some serious egg on their face, and Annie was questioned about who the mysterious gunman might be. She said only, "Well, he must have been a very bad man,"[56] apparently with a straight face.

Initially, the local press identified the "very bad man" as Robert Leroy Parker, better known as Butch Cassidy. In hindsight, it couldn't have been him; Cassidy was on the run in South America at the time the "Ice Wagon Man" ran amok in Nashville. It wouldn't be until April 1902 that the suspect was identified after he was shot dead by police in a San Antonio bordello. He turned out to be Orlando C. "Deaf Charley" Hanks, one of the three Wagner train robbers. The second, Ben Kilpatrick, was picked up in St. Louis on November 5, 1901, and later sentenced to federal prison. Then, on December 13, Harvey Logan shot two police officers during a bar fight in Knoxville and was arrested two days later. The gang was officially out of business.

Annie quietly awaited her fate in Nashville, still insisting that she never knew the money was stolen and that she didn't know the man who gave it to her. Her story took a heavy hit at a hearing for bail reduction in April when Pinkerton detective Lowell Spence revealed a photo taken from Harvey Logan's watch after his arrest in Knoxville. It showed Annie and Harvey, side by side, her arm resting familiarly on his shoulder. Things were looking bad for her, but she had an ace in the hole.

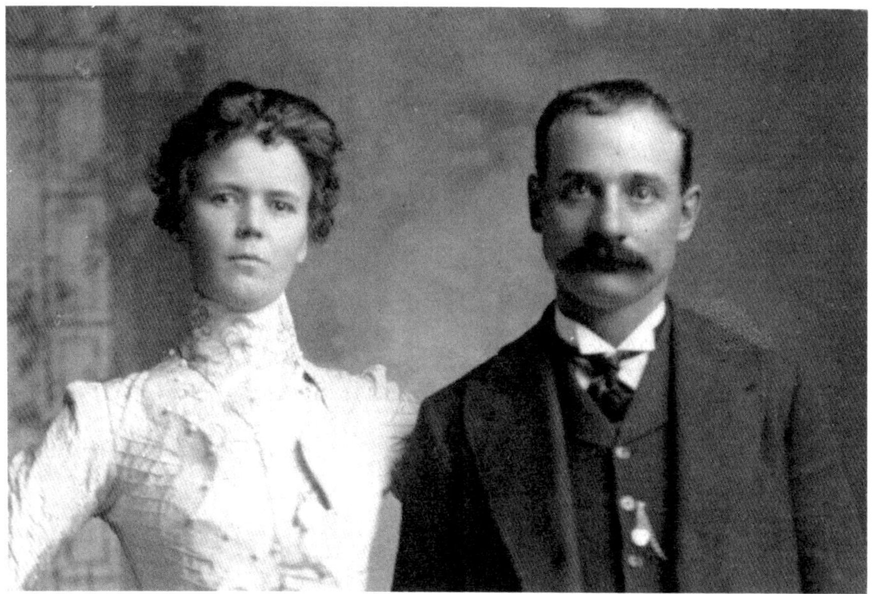

A copy of this photo, showing Annie and Harvey Logan together, was recovered from Logan's watch case after his arrest, showing that she had a long association with the bad man. *National Archives.*

When she appeared for her trial on June 14, 1902, Annie looked haggard and pale from her long confinement. When a reporter asked her if she was getting tired, she sighed and replied that "she had been tired since the day she was arrested."[57] However, she wasn't defenseless. To the surprise of many, her lawyer, Richard West, was accompanied by William H. Washington, a high-powered former district attorney. Even more surprising, their fees were being paid by Morgan Roop, a local cigar merchant, who claimed he did so just because he felt sorry for the defendant. He later testified that the Pinkertons had threatened him to get him to drop the case and even had him followed to see if he was a go-between for Annie and Logan's gang. They found no evidence of any wrongdoing. Incredibly, it seems as if Roop really was Annie's knight in shining armor.

Her defense predictably leaned on the fact that in that era twelve *men* had to sit in judgment over whether this attractive young woman was one of the most dangerous gun molls in America or simply a victim of circumstance. They hammered at errors in procedure and got the police to admit on the stand that Annie had been misled into making statements without being informed that she should have an attorney present. She also turned on "Happy Jack" Dwyer, now claiming that he had been abusive to her at the station after her arrest and that she'd been forced to submit to a strip search. When she took the stand in her own defense, her customary defiance was reflected in her flamboyant wardrobe—a pale green shirtwaist with a lavender scarf that covered her entire bosom, a black skirt and a straw hat trimmed in green velvet with a feather stuck in it. She answered questions "briskly" and made "an excellent witness," not deviating from her original story in the face of stiff questioning by the prosecution.[58]

The state presented little evidence proving she knew who Harvey Logan was or that she knew the money was tainted. On June 18, 1902, after only an hour and a half of deliberation, the jury foreman made his announcement: "We find the defendant not guilty." He smiled broadly as he spoke, and applause exploded in the courtroom. Annie shook hands with her attorney, the judge and every member of the jury as bystanders congratulated her. The notorious outlaw's woman had won the sympathy of the citizens of Nashville.

Annie stuck around for a short while, living on the largesse of her friend Roop. She wrote to Logan once or twice, telling him that she wished she could see him but the notoriety attached to her wouldn't help his case. "You must believe I've been a good girl for you ever since I've been released….I know we will be together soon."[59] She was quite wrong. Later that year, Logan was convicted of the Wagner holdup. Sentenced to twenty years in prison, he never served a day. In the summer of 1903, he staged a spectacular breakout from the Knoxville jail and fled back to his old stomping grounds, boasting that now that he was free "there'll be hell to pay!" But just a year later, he held up a train at Parachute, Colorado, and on June 7, 1904, wounded and trapped by a pursuing posse, he called to his partners, "I'm all in and might as well end it right here." Then he shot himself.[60]

Annie didn't go quietly either. Following her acquittal, she pulled a move that proved she had as much brass as any member of the Wild Bunch: she sued the federal government for the return of the money. Arguing that she had been acquitted of wrongdoing and that she earned it fairly, she requested the $550 be turned back over to her. The case took a year to come to conclusion, but when it did, the result was predictable. The court found that regardless of how she came by them, the bills were "forcibly taken by highway robbers," which was proven at her trial and negated her claims of being "an innocent 'holder'" of the money.[61] Case dismissed. At any rate, you can't blame her for trying.

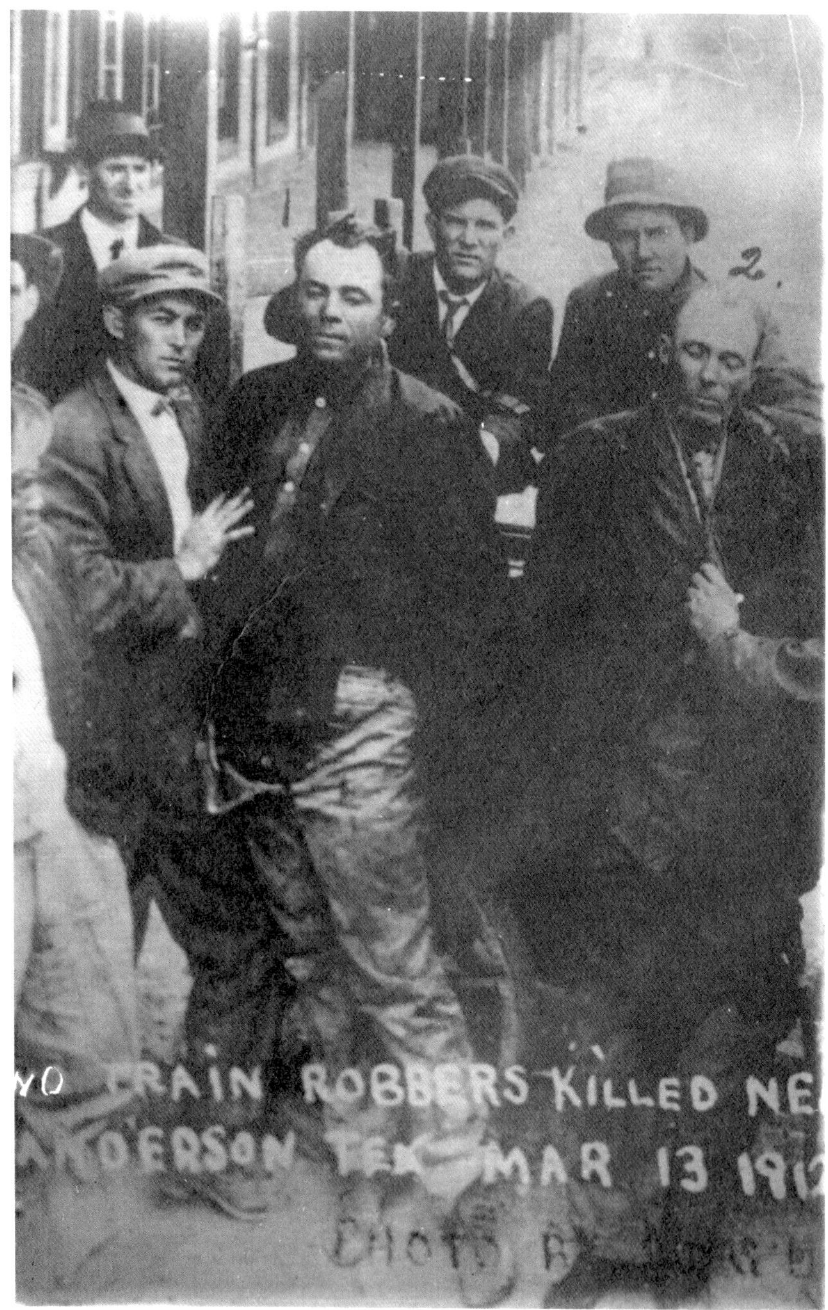

None of the Montana robbers came to a good end. Last to go was Ben Kilpatrick (*left*), who was killed in 1912 while robbing a train at Sanderson, Texas. *Library of Congress.*

By the time the decision was handed down in December 1903, Annie was "in far-away Texas" and "living a quiet and peaceable life."[62] Just how long that life remained quiet is hard to say, but she soon fell back into the path she knew best. By May 1906, the Pinkertons reported her working once more as a prostitute, living in a room over Dee Picci's saloon in Hot Springs, Arkansas. There was one more dubious sighting of her in 1908 near Lander, Wyoming, and then all trace of Annie Rogers went completely cold.

Where she went after that is anyone's guess. One unverifiable rumor has it she became a schoolteacher and died around 1926, but given her record and her lifestyle, that's probably too romantic to be true. In a way, perhaps it's better not to know for sure. In her prime she lived by her wits, and unlike most of her associates, she actually got away scot free. Just like the hero of a classic Western, she blazed across the landscape before disappearing into the sunset, leaving a colorful legend behind. And somehow that seems the most fitting way for her saga to end.

CHAPTER 7

LADY IN THE WATER

Looking at its all but deserted streets today, you would never guess that Cairo, Illinois, was once one of the busiest ports on the Ohio River, servicing passengers and trade from across the country. Appropriately, it was the murky waters of the river that delivered a truly puzzling mystery to the city's waterfront on the afternoon of January 25, 1906—a mystery with its origins hundreds of miles to the east.

A watchman on shore saw what appeared to be a human body floating by, and the tugboat *Theseus* moved to intercept. The corpse was towed to the shore near the Illinois Central Railroad bridge, and the coroner was called. The body proved to be that of a woman, and despite the fact that she had been in the water for a considerable time, she was evidently a "once beautiful young lady."[63]

A full post-mortem was carried out at the morgue and an inventory taken of her effects. Some of her clothing had come away in the water, but what remained was of excellent quality: a tattered grayish-blue wool overskirt, a silk underskirt, black stockings, a silk corset and high-top laced shoes. She was five feet, six inches tall, around 125 pounds and around thirty years old, and wisps of blond hair still hung about her head although almost all of her scalp was gone. There were signs of foul play: her garters had been cut, and one of her stockings had been pulled halfway off. There was no jewelry or cash on the body. An inflatable pair of rubber "breast inflaters," meant to "improve" the figure, was fastened around the torso. Like a life vest, they had helped the remains stay afloat for some time.

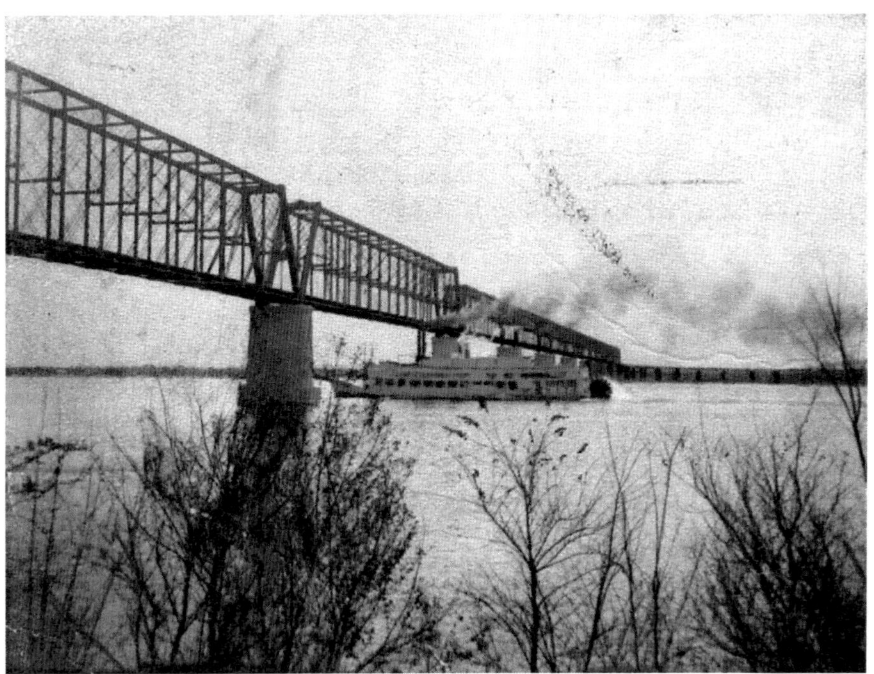

The L&N Railroad bridge over the Ohio River at Cairo, Illinois. Close to this spot a mysterious body drifted to shore in 1906, sparking a sensational murder mystery hundreds of miles away in Nashville. *Author's collection.*

The shoes bore the imprint of Kuhn, Cooper & Geary of Nashville, serial number 8323. The firm was contacted and checked its ledgers. It had no record of that number, it said, but it had sold a pair numbered 8823 to Mrs. Rosa Mangrum of 302 Sixth Avenue North.

With that, a mystery was solved and a new one developed. Mrs. Mangrum had been missing since December 14, 1905, when she had supposedly boarded a northbound train at Union Station to visit family in Chicago. Her sister and husband had reported her missing at the time, but how she ended up in the river at Cairo was anybody's guess. Mrs. Mangrum's sister, Florence Mason, and her husband, Oscar, traveled to Cairo, where they soon confirmed that the body was Rosa's. Then the press began looking into the matter, and soon some interesting facts came to light.

Rosa Mason was born in Jackson, Tennessee, in 1872 and moved to Nashville as a young woman, finding work with the Eclipse Manufacturing Company. In 1896 she married James Oscar Mangrum, a barber, but the marriage doesn't seem to have been a happy one. At the time of her disappearance, she lived separately from her husband at a boardinghouse. Unusual for the time, Rosa traveled frequently by herself, organizing charity concerts in other cities. In fact, she had just returned from one such trip at the time she left for Chicago.

December 14 was a rainy, cold night. Mrs. Mangrum had purchased tickets, including accommodations in a Pullman sleeping car. She sent for a hack to pick up her luggage and told her husband that he needn't see her off at the station, instead telling him to go back and close up his shop for the night. At 7:45 p.m. she reached Union Station, just fifteen minutes before her train was due to depart. She made a phone call to an unknown party at 7:50 and was last seen heading through the gate just afterward. The train departed exactly at 8:00 p.m.

And this is where things get hazy. Nobody aboard the train remembered seeing her, and certainly she never slept in the Pullman, leaving doubt whether she actually got on board. Stranger still, she had told her husband she was heading for Chicago, but in a letter to her sister she said she intended going to St. Louis first to visit her friend Mabel Luttrell—a fact she never mentioned to her husband. It was confirmed that she'd asked for her mail to be forwarded to the Lorraine Hotel in St. Louis but had sent her trunk on to Chicago, where it was later found. Apparently, she had intended to visit St. Louis without a change of clothing.

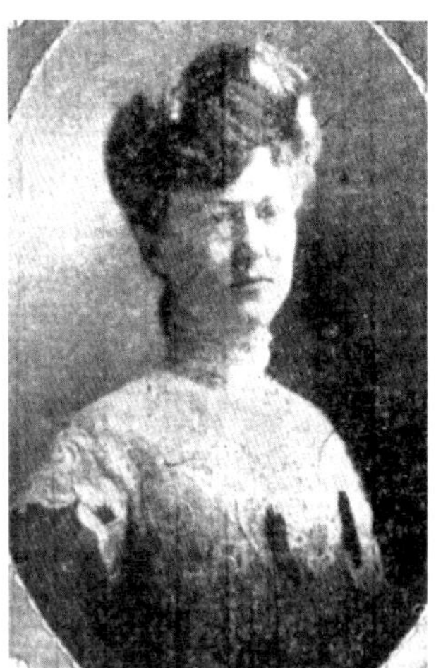

Rosa Mangrum in her only known photograph, which ran in the local papers after her death. *Courtesy Tennessee State Library and Archives.*

More alarming, she had left home with all her worldly possessions, including $1,500 in cash, which she kept in her stocking, and five diamond and ruby rings worth $1,200 on her left hand. Her missing left glove and the cut garters indicated that someone had robbed her before she went into the river.

The remains were sent to Nashville, where a more extensive autopsy was held. The results were disturbing. While the doctors found no sign of injury or poison, they became convinced that her hair had been removed deliberately, rather than by the action of the river. They also ruled out drowning as the cause of death, making suicide or accident most unlikely.

As puzzling as how she died was how she ended up where she was found. One theory had it she'd been murdered at Nashville and dumped in the river. But the body would have had to drift 250 miles down the Cumberland to the Ohio and then to Cairo. Given the six-week time span, it was theoretically possible, but there were several locks and dams below the city that should have prevented this. And despite the heavily traveled waters, no reliable sighting of the corpse was found along the whole route. Because of this, some thought she'd been killed along her travel route, possibly at Jeffersonville, Indiana.

For weeks the case seemed to stall. And then all at once there was a sensational bombshell. Oscar Mangrum and Florence Mason had insisted all along that one person was responsible, and the authorities looked hard at this suspect, but for obvious reasons they had to be sure before they moved. On March 16, 1906, Detective Robert Sidebottom and two other officers walked into the office of Dr. J. Herman Feist and quietly told him he was under arrest for murder. Feist, a prominent Nashville medical man, offered no protest. He contacted his attorney before accompanying the policemen to the station.

Jacob Herman Feist was no stranger to controversy. On the surface, he was a respected doctor with a lifestyle befitting a successful practice. He dressed well and had an office in the upscale Wilcox Building (now Cornerstone Square). However, when this image of respectability was scraped, it flaked away, and a far less flattering picture emerged.

Born in Alabama in 1873, he was the son of Alsatian German immigrants who studied in New York and Europe before receiving his medical degree at the University of Tennessee. Despite his fashionable location, his practice was less than successful, and Feist was perpetually in debt. He seemed to get by on appearances.

Feist had a natural charisma, and one friend recalled him as a "spellbinder."[64] He was a strikingly handsome man with thick dark hair and a neat moustache, along with a vanity to match. His practice seemed to chiefly consist of pretty ladies from all walks of life, and in the short time he'd been working in Nashville he had acquired an unenviable reputation as a lothario. Worse yet, this wasn't the first time a lady linked to him had ended up dead.

In 1897, he was treating Mrs. Martha Swan for Bright's disease. Some noticed that during his frequent visits to her home he was paying undue attention to her striking eighteen-year-old daughter, Mary. On June 18, 1898, Virgil Swan, then fifteen, came home to find his mother deathly ill in the garden behind the house. He called Dr. Feist, who gave her an injection, but Mrs. Swan slipped into a coma and died two hours later.

After her death, it was found that she had taken out $5,000 in life insurance in Dr. Feist's name, supposedly as security for medical bills she knew she'd never be able to pay. When the surviving children threatened legal action against the doctor, he agreed to take only his fees out of the settlement, giving the remainder to them, and the affair ended quietly.

Four years later, an even more dramatic incident occurred when twenty-three-year-old Sadie Goldstein, an "unusually pretty" secretary working for the Cumberland Telephone Company, committed suicide in the Wilcox Building.[65] At around 6:30 p.m. on May 9, 1903, Sadie phoned her sister Pearl, asking her to meet her at Feist's office. She was obviously under the influence and admitted to Pearl that she'd swallowed twenty-two half-grain morphine tablets. There are two versions of what happened next.

In his official statement, Feist claimed he knew the girl casually and had no idea why she'd come to his office, but when he realized her distress he worked heroically all through the night to save her life, calling several other doctors in to aid him. He thought when she was removed from his office the following morning that she was on her way to recovery and was more surprised than anyone when she died—implying his fellow physicians must have done something wrong. "We could not understand why she did not recover," he said, "every indication pointing to her recovery." Rather insensitively, he added an afterthought: "I regret very much the publicity given to it."[66]

The following day came a rebuttal from Sadie's family. She had been having an affair with him, they said, and when she caught him with another woman, she confronted him. In response, he angrily ordered her out of his office before leaving in a huff. That's when she swallowed the morphine. When Feist returned, he claimed she was faking and coldly refused to treat her, leaving her gasping on his couch in the care of her family as he left once more.

Three hours later, he eventually returned when another family member tracked him down. Finally acknowledging that something was wrong, he reluctantly began treating her, giving her an injection that he later said was an emetic to make her throw up. As emetics are generally given orally, and as Sadie was still capable of swallowing, it's a curiously suspect explanation. Sadie's family thought he'd given an extra dose of morphine to finish her off.

Only when the family called in another doctor did Feist snap out of his funk and actively begin to treat her symptoms. Throughout the night the doctors labored, but incredibly, at nine o'clock the next morning, Feist told

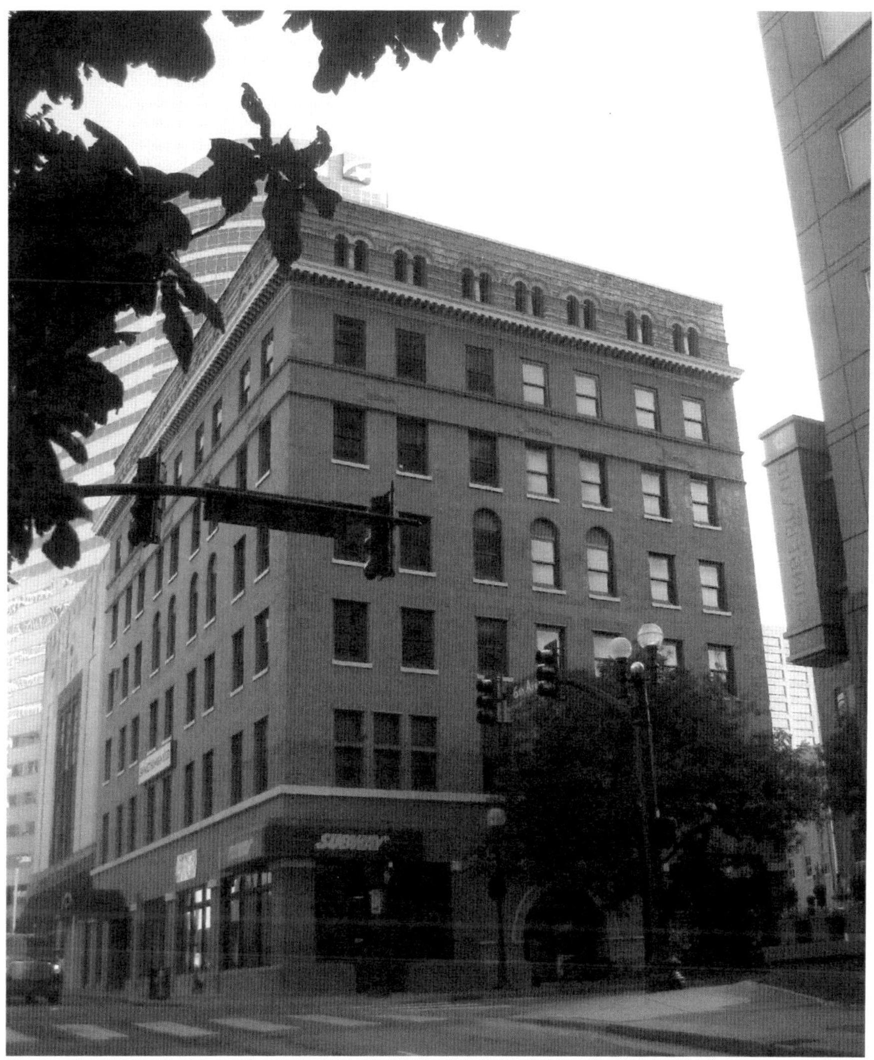

The Wilcox Building still stands today on the corner of Sixth Avenue and Church Street. Dr. Feist had an office here where some of the sensational events surrounding the case played out. *Author's photograph.*

them to move the girl out of his office because he had to open for business. The other doctor, Walter Lenehan, had her moved to a private sanitarium run by Dr. Richard Douglas on Peabody Street, where she died an hour later. Dr. Douglas later rebutted Feist's statement that Sadie was recovering, saying that "the young lady was in a hopeless condition and actually dying when I first saw her."[67]

According to her family, young Sadie was hopelessly infatuated with Feist and spent her meager paycheck on purchasing furniture for his swanky new office at the Wilcox—the very furniture on which she died. Feist lamely explained her purchases as payment for medical services and said he'd repaid her for the furniture, without explaining why he'd taken such an unconventional method of payment in the first place. The family threatened to prosecute, but in the end, there wasn't enough evidence, and no charges were filed. Sadie Goldstein was quietly laid to rest in the Temple Ohabai Sholom Cemetery, and Feist resumed his practice.

Now another of his "patients" was dead under mysterious conditions. Rosa Mangrum had first started seeing him for treatment in 1904, and for a while, all seemed normal. Eventually, her husband became suspicious and confronted his wife. "She said there was nothing wrong in the visits," Mangrum recalled, "and refused to discontinue them."[68]

They continued to be a source of friction though, and Rosa finally agreed to stop visiting Feist. However, Oscar Mangrum later discovered that despite her promises, Rosa was still going to the Wilcox regularly. To her sister Florence, Rosa admitted that "she was in love with a Nashville physician," adding, "He has the strangest influence over me. I do not understand it, Florence. He makes me dislike Oscar.…He wants me to elope with him.…I long to see him, and yet I am afraid."[69] Of what, she didn't say. She also said she'd loaned Feist over $300. According to her last letter, Rosa planned to go to Chicago and file for divorce so that she could marry Dr. Feist.

The embattled doctor denied everything—albeit in a tone-deaf, selfish manner. "It is humiliating to be accused of murder and robbery for the paltry sum of $1500. I don't look like a murderer, do I?" he asked a reporter, leaving the reader wondering what sum he would have considered reasonable.[70] At his preliminary hearing he was laughing and joking with his friends—that is, until Rosa's father, J.E. Mason of Jackson, Tennessee, tried to attack him in the courtroom. Mason wasn't armed and was convinced to leave after a scuffle, but the incident seemed to sober the defendant. He maintained his innocence throughout.

The case the state put forward was classic Victorian hyperbole. The virtuous Mrs. Mangrum, they maintained, had been led astray by her handsome seducer, who then robbed and murdered her. They even produced a witness who swore he saw a blacked-out carriage parked near a manhole on the night she disappeared. The two occupants of the vehicle dropped something into the sewer before hurrying away—obviously the body of the murdered woman, they theorized. High water had then taken her over the falls below the city and washed her up in Illinois. However, the cause of death was unclear, and there was precious little physical evidence to suggest a homicide had even occurred.

On April 4, the grand jury handed down an indictment for murder. Feist's attorneys argued that the $10,000 bond proposed was excessive, but the judge overruled them. Unprepared to pay such a fee, Feist failed to give bond and was remanded to jail. His protests against being lodged like a common prisoner fell on deaf ears, and he was placed in a "cage" on the lowest level of the building, where he would remain until trial.

His treatment appears to have shaken him. He had earlier promised to release another statement for the press, but when a reporter came to see him, he remained silent. "Almost petulantly he answered…'See my attorneys,'"[71] before abruptly ending the interview.

Public opinion remained divided. Some saw him as a suave Svengali and serial seducer, but Feist also had many powerful friends. When his bond was reduced to $1,000, at least seven prominent men stepped forward to sign it. As might have been expected with such a cast of characters, the attorneys on both sides prepared themselves for a titanic court battle.

On January 24, 1907, the epic trial got underway, and it was as contentious as the press hoped. From the beginning, the defense came out swinging, chipping away at the lack of physical evidence and casting doubt on witnesses. When Oscar Mangrum took the stand to testify about his wife's infidelities, the defense team came back at him with accusations that he'd been seen with other girls around town. And, they pointed out, since his wife's death, he had married a second time with what appeared to be unseemly haste.

The prosecution came back with equally salacious details. Mabel McCain, a lady of the evening, was called to testify about an incident she said took place at an infamous "house of assignation" run by Grace Chester. The house, notorious in Nashville, was a place where couples could go when they wanted…discretion. Mabel said that a few days before Mrs. Mangrum vanished, she heard voices coming from a neighboring room—a man who was talking to "Rosa, dear Rosa," and a woman whose voice she recognized as that of Mrs. Mangrum. She couldn't make out the bulk of the conversation, but at one point she heard Rosa address him as "Herman Feist" and tell him that "she saw no reason to carry that amount with her." The defense dragged her over the coals, implying that she was being paid or threatened for her testimony. The exchange was described as "very sensational at times"[72] and became heated enough that the judge threatened to start issuing fines if both sides didn't stop shooting one-liners at each other. However, the defense did tear Mabel apart on cross-examination, catching her in more than a dozen lies or exaggerations.

The state scored enough points that the judge increased Feist's bond to $10,000 once more. By the time his defense team began its argument, public interest had exploded. The courtroom was standing room only, and the crowds spilled into the corridors as the somewhat contradictory testimony continued.

The doctors who conducted the autopsy shed no further light on the cause of death, ruling out strangling, drowning, disease or trauma—all injuries on the corpse were inflicted post-mortem. The prevailing theory was that some sort of poison may have caused death, but since the remains were embalmed in Cairo before the Nashville autopsy, the results of any such examination would be questionable at best. Doctors called by the defense pointed out that after forty-five days in the water it would be extremely difficult to determine whether she drowned.

There were stories about a floating body sighted at McClee's ferry... which admittedly may have been a log. There were tales of shadowy men in blacked-out carriages who may or may not have looked like Feist, seen

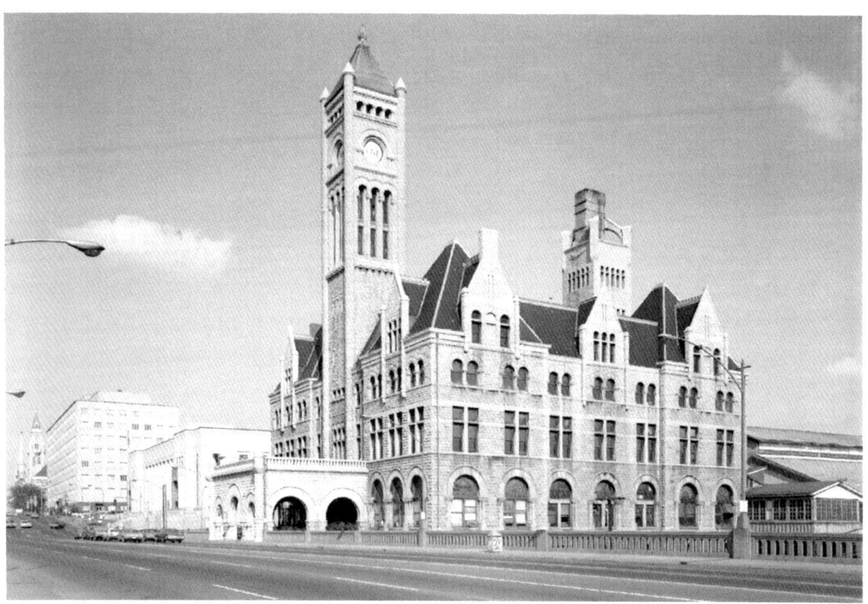

Scene of the crime? The last reliable sighting of Rosa Mangrum took place here at Union Station on Broadway. The building still stands today and is now a hotel. *Library of Congress.*

picking up a woman who could have been Mrs. Mangrum at Union Station the night she disappeared. On the other hand, Feist had a strong alibi. Several witnesses testified that the doctor had eaten supper with Abe Bloomstein's family on the night of the crime. At the time Mrs. Mangrum boarded the train, Dr. Feist was seated in front of several witnesses in a fashionable dining room. Dora Bloomstein distinctly recalled speaking to him that night about the death of his father and whether he intended to pay his respects with traditional ceremony.

As the defense strongly pointed out in its closing argument, all the evidence in the case was circumstantial. There was no real proof a murder had even been committed, let alone that the defendant had done it. It wasn't even clear whether or not Mrs. Mangrum had been aboard the train that night. "I say it is slop," attorney K.T. McConnico bluntly stated, "and I say that no jury can take this slop and mess and analyze it into proof to put a man to death."[73]

It had been a grueling, three-week ordeal—long enough that several members of the jury came down sick from sitting in the freezing courtroom. They filed out to deliberate on February 15, and they were back the next day to render their verdict: guilty of murder in the first degree. There was a stunned silence in the courtroom, and Feist wilted in his seat. With preternatural calm, the judge thanked the jury and dismissed them as the sheriff took custody of the defendant. Evidently, the state's "slop" had indeed been enough to convict a man of murder. The crowd cheered as the disgraced doctor was escorted back to jail in handcuffs. He muttered that it appeared all of his friends had deserted him. In his cell, he was placed on a suicide watch.

However, his defense team was not done yet, and a motion was filed for a new trial. The hearing was almost as dramatic as the original case, dragging on for over a week while sensational accusations were made by Feist's attorneys. Among the most startling testimony came from the bellboys at the Commercial Hotel who had delivered a gallon of whiskey a day to the room where the jury was sequestered. Four of the jury testified that they hadn't touched the stuff. "That leaves eight men to get rid of four quarts a day," commented one editor. "The man that can drink a pint of 'fire water' in a day and not be effected [*sic*] by it must be old at the business."[74]

But despite the charges of a drunken jury and other irregularities, the motion for a new trial was denied. Feist's attorneys immediately began prepping the case for an appeal to the Supreme Court while the doctor's friends made an effort to keep him comfortable during his long confinement,

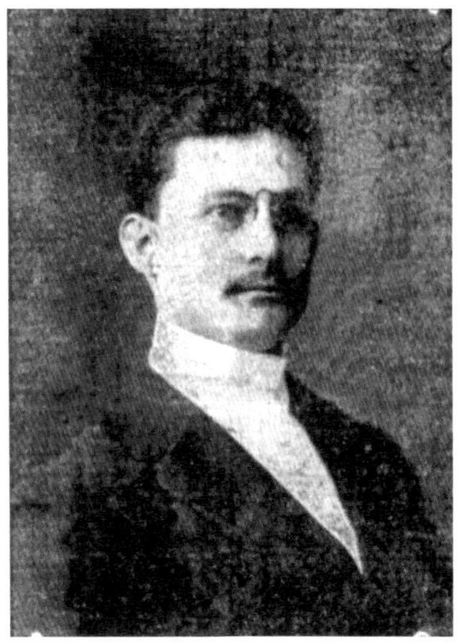

Dr. J. Herman Feist was a figurative lady-killer, but was he also one literally? That was the question put before a jury at his high-profile murder trial. *Courtesy Tennessee State Library and Archives.*

even hanging wallpaper in his cell to cheer him. The paper had a ribbon design on it, and attorney McConnico remarked that he thought it was in poor taste. When Feist asked him why, he replied, "Why, don't you see, Doctor? Ropes!" "Since the sentence was death by hanging at that time, this suggestion...did not seem pleasing to Dr. Feist," recalled one of McConnico's associates.[75] He spent his days listening to the less-than-cheering sound of hammers and saws constructing the gallows in the jail yard.

His attorneys refused to give up, and eventually the Supreme Court heard their appeal. They sided with the defense that the evidence in the case was weak in the extreme, and Feist was finally granted a retrial. In the spring of 1908, after posting $25,000 bond, he was allowed to go home to Alabama. His health was a wreck after a year in jail, and many thought he would never live to see his day in court.

They were wrong, though. Pale, haggard and with far more gray in his hair, he was present as his next ordeal opened in June 1909. In the three years since the first go-around, the state had hunted high and low but still had no additional evidence, and this time the defense was ready for them. With little ado, the jury returned a verdict of not guilty, and J. Herman Feist was finally a free man.

His near-death experience had taken its toll, however. "He is greatly changed in outward appearances," one reporter noted, "and many...would scarcely recognize him in his present condition."[76] Haunted by his past, his career in tatters, Feist lost no time in leaving the city that had shattered him and retired to his native Alabama, where he settled near Bay Minette.

He returned once or twice on sundry matters, looking far more frail and subdued than he did in his prime. Local legend wanted to believe that he had later gone insane in remorse over his deeds and died a miserable death. In fact, his end was sad, but with more than a hint of redemption. Denied the right to practice medicine in Alabama, he did so anyway, as the community around Tensaw needed a doctor and he was the only one available. On several occasions he was brought to trial for practicing without a license, but he was acquitted each time due to public pressure.

An hour after he was sentenced to die, Feist had told a reporter, "You tell that old red-nosed judge I will outlive him."[77] He was good as his word, surviving his trial judge by more than four decades, but he was never the same man. His trial aged him and cured him of his skirt-chasing. He never married and lived as a bachelor for the rest of his life with only a housekeeper as his companion. Late in life, at the request of his neighbors, he was granted the dignity of a medical license to practice only within Baldwin County. He died on October 16, 1952, at the age of seventy-nine and was buried in Montgomery Hill Cemetery.

Looking back with more than a century of hindsight, it's hard to see Feist as a completely innocent victim. Almost certainly he was a serial womanizer and quite possibly a swindler. He was arrogant and reckless, and his brash attitude set him up as a likely suspect when Rosa Mangrum died. But was he really a killer? That's harder to say.

Certainly, his behavior with Mrs. Swan and Sadie Goldstein looks suspicious, but neither case ever came to trial. Almost certainly Rosa Mangrum died suspiciously—either by her own hand or someone else's—but the evidence presented in court was useless to the point of laughable. If she was indeed murdered, little hard evidence was introduced tying the doctor to the crime. It remains a distinct possibility that some thief noticed Mrs. Mangrum's money on the train and chloroformed her for it before dumping her body in the river. Suicide or accident were also possibilities, but the prosecution seemed bore sighted on Feist from the beginning and never pursued any alternative theories. It seems he was tried and convicted based on his unsavory reputation alone, and in that respect, one can only call what happened to him a gross miscarriage of justice.

But then again, nobody ever accused Nashville's courts of being predictable. Seven years after Mrs. Mangrum's mysterious end, an even more salacious affair took place, resulting in one of the most shocking scenes in Tennessee legal history.

CHAPTER 8

HELL HATH NO FURY

On the sunny afternoon of March 15, 1913, a slender, pretty young blond woman stepped off a day train at Union Station. She was dressed in a fashionable brown walking dress with the typical large hat pinned to her upswept hair. Her hands were shielded from the spring chill by a fur muff. Her expression was set and determined as she strode out of the station and down the street two blocks until she came to the door of Jackson's barbershop on Broadway.

The place was crowded—four customers in chairs, two waiting and two more getting a shine from the bootblacks. In that day, a barbershop was an almost exclusively male environment, and several customers looked up in surprise as she walked in. She obviously didn't have a son or husband with her, which was unusual. Some thought she looked vaguely familiar.

Jackson's was an upscale joint gleaming with marble and mahogany, smelling of talc and bay rum, the barbers dressed in neat white coats. The woman approached one of them, a new hire named Charlie Cobb, who was finishing with a customer in chair number four, dusting him off with a brush. S.H. McHurdy, the barber at the neighboring station, looked up in time to see Cobb smile and nod at her in a friendly manner. The woman's face, on the other hand, was a mask of stone. Like a scene from a play, they exchanged a long, significant look as she stepped to within three feet of him. Neither said a word.

Then the woman withdrew her right hand from the muff, clutching a .32-caliber Smith & Wesson revolver, which she pointed at Cobb's head.

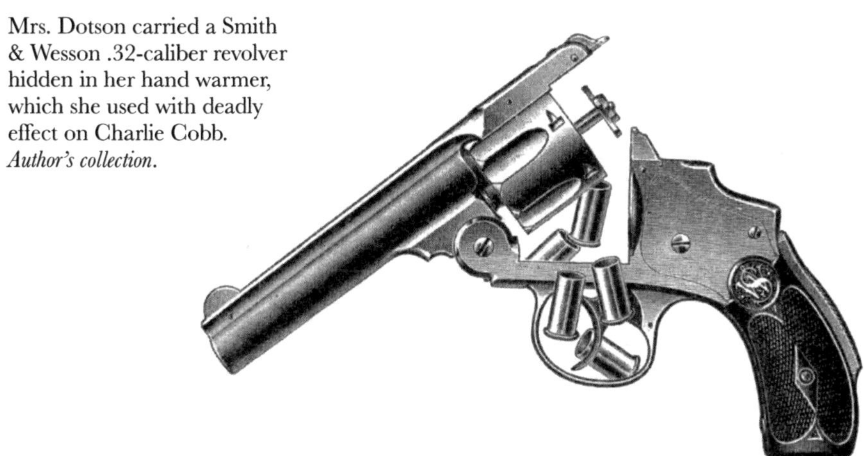

Mrs. Dotson carried a Smith & Wesson .32-caliber revolver hidden in her hand warmer, which she used with deadly effect on Charlie Cobb. *Author's collection.*

Four rapid shots filled the air with smoke, and the barber, his white coat and face blackened by powder burns and spattered with blood, teetered for a second before collapsing against his chair. The woman stared at him "with fascinated eyes."

The shots blasted the calm atmosphere into splinters, and within moments, many of the customers were at least half a block away, running like sheep. The one Cobb had been shaving hit the door with a towel stuffed in his shirt and never came back to get his collar or necktie. The authorities never identified him.

C.A. Hodges, another barber, stood wide-eyed and frozen in shock. The woman noticed him and then calmly turned to him. "He ruined my home, and wrecked my life," she said, and then coolly asked what she should do. She was told to sit down and wait, that the police were surely coming. She took a seat, remarking, "I have done what I came down to do."[78] But when she noticed Cobb gasping and struggling to rise, she said, "I don't believe he is dead yet" and pointed her pistol at the victim on the floor.[79] Bystanders grabbed her and twisted it out of her hand before she could fire again.

The wounded Cobb was bundled into an automobile outside that chugged its way to the City Hospital, one and a half miles distant. He arrived a little past four o'clock, and the staff immediately wheeled him in, attaching him to the new pulmotor machine to try to resuscitate him. It was too late. He died without regaining consciousness at 4:15 p.m., about forty-five minutes after he was shot. Doctors later ascertained that he'd been hit three times. One had clipped his left ear and neck, while the two killing shots had hit him in the base of the skull and in the left side, grazing the heart. He was thirty-one years old. Charlie's body went to the morgue as the authorities tracked down his wife to tell her what had happened. She was out of town in Kentucky at the time, so the news was broken to her by a long-distance telephone call.

Meanwhile, back at the shop, the woman made no effort to run or to hide her identity. She was thirty-two-year-old Anna Dotson, the wife of Dr. Walter S. Dotson, a physician from nearby Gallatin, Tennessee. Within a few minutes, Chief of Detectives Robert J. Sidebottom arrived along with the paddy wagon and placed her under arrest. Mrs. Dotson was driven to the Central Police Station and booked, after which she was placed into a cell in the women's section, where she continually paced the floor, tears streaking her face.

When a reporter arrived and asked why she'd done such a thing, the answer she gave was surprising. "I did not do it for revenge," she said. "I shot him to protect my brother and husband. I was afraid that they would kill him, and I did not want anyone to suffer for my sins."[80] Her voice was flat and emotionless.

Born Sarah Anna Dennis in Jackson, Tennessee, on April 24, 1880, she'd lived a fairly quiet life up until that time. A preacher's daughter, she married her husband at the age of seventeen. He was two years older and

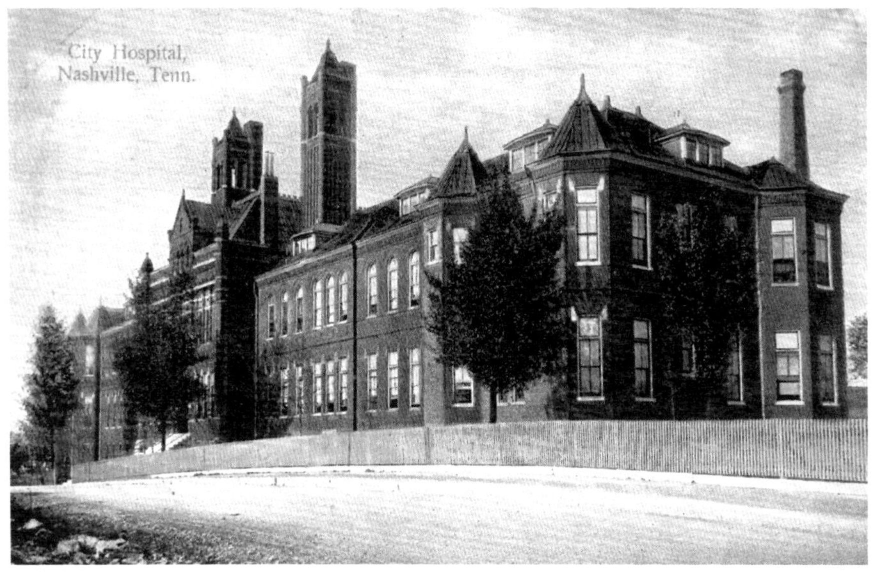

City Hospital, where Cobb was taken after his shooting. Desperate efforts were made to save him, but to no avail. The building still stands today on Middleton Street. *Author's collection.*

studying for his medical degree. After graduation, he became an ear, nose and throat specialist, and they moved to the small town of Kempville so he could start his practice. In 1907, they moved to Gallatin. The couple had a daughter and a son together, and on the surface, she was playing the part of the dutiful Christian wife and mother, but behind the scenes, there were tensions building. Anna had been inexperienced with the opposite sex before her marriage, recalling that "she was not permitted to have company by her parents."[81] Married life left her feeling stifled and lonely. Her husband proved distant and lost in his work. "I thought that my husband did not love me," she remembered, "he did not show any sympathy or seem to care."[82] The family moved to Gallatin when her husband found a new practice. He either didn't notice her frustrations or couldn't cope with them, and by 1911, the couple was drifting apart.

On a Sunday afternoon in July of that year, she was sitting on her front porch reading the paper, chatting with her sister and her children. Dr. Dotson, as was often the case, was away on business. That's when a young man with dark curly hair and a bright smile opened the gate and strode boldly up to where she sat. She didn't know him, but she thought he was attractive the moment she laid eyes on him. The stranger raised his hat politely and asked if he could borrow her newspaper. She handed it to him, and he left for a short time, returning with it a little later. He struck up a conversation with Anna, chatting about religion and how lonely his Sundays were since his wife was out of town. He told her he lived at the Keystone Hotel across the street and said they'd met once before, while Anna was quite sure they hadn't. The whole encounter was shockingly forward for the times and left her flustered.

When her husband returned, she mentioned the unsettling encounter to him, but Dotson brushed it off. That was just Charlie Cobb, he said, and that was the way he was—"he was known to be very familiar." Indeed he was. Soon, Charlie was timing his visits suspiciously, and Anna was encouraging him to do so. Whenever Dr. Dotson left for another call, Cobb would drop by to see Anna. "In a few months we had become very good friends." That was a delicate way of putting it.

Perhaps it was just human nature. Anna was immature, high-spirited and starved for excitement and attention. Charlie was gregarious and charming, with a humorous disposition that made him very popular in town. He was married himself with a little daughter, but he had a roving eye, and the doctor's wife and the barber were soon enmeshed in an affair that became an open secret in Gallatin.

They lived dangerously. Charlie even introduced his wife to Anna, and both couples came to frequent the Dotson home. Daisy Cobb later recalled bitterly that Anna Dotson "was my most intimate friend"[83] during that time. But even as they played cards, went to the cinema and listened to the gramophone together, Anna was sending postcards to Charlie, such as the following from August 1911:

> *Saturday afternoon*
> *At home.*
> *Say; I will be home all afternoon* <u>*alone*</u>*. All have gone to the fair but me. "Guess!" and I am lonely.*
> *P.S. No one suspicions anything.*[84]

It appears that the only two in town who didn't seem to know about the affair were Dr. Dotson and Mrs. Cobb. Before long, Anna recalled, when she walked the sidewalk with her unsuspecting husband, friends began giving her knowing looks, "and I could not look them in the face."[85] It couldn't last forever, and in February 1913, it all blew up. Walter discovered the affair, and Anna admitted everything.

The doctor took it badly. According to Anna's version, he promptly grabbed a pistol and headed uptown, looking for Cobb. He extracted a confession at gunpoint and then told him that if Cobb left town immediately, he wouldn't kill him. Charlie's old boss in Gallatin remembered that the evening before, Cobb and Dr. Dotson had been best friends, playing checkers and laughing together. The very next morning, Dotson coldly informed him that Cobb would not be coming back. When he asked why his favorite employee had suddenly left town, Dotson glared in such a way that he quickly dropped the subject. Cobb went to Nashville, where he took the job at Jackson's.

When Dotson came home, Anna said there was a ferocious row, during which he tried to kill her or himself and the gun went off accidentally. She said that Walter told her he'd never forgive her for not confessing sooner and that if he ever saw Cobb again he'd kill him. Further, the scandal would blacken their name in town and above all, he wanted their children to be shielded from the fallout. He was taking the kids to Westmoreland, he said, and she was going to Texas. He wanted her as far from them as possible. She was devastated.

Then, suddenly, she went to Nashville to get a haircut for her son at Jackson's.

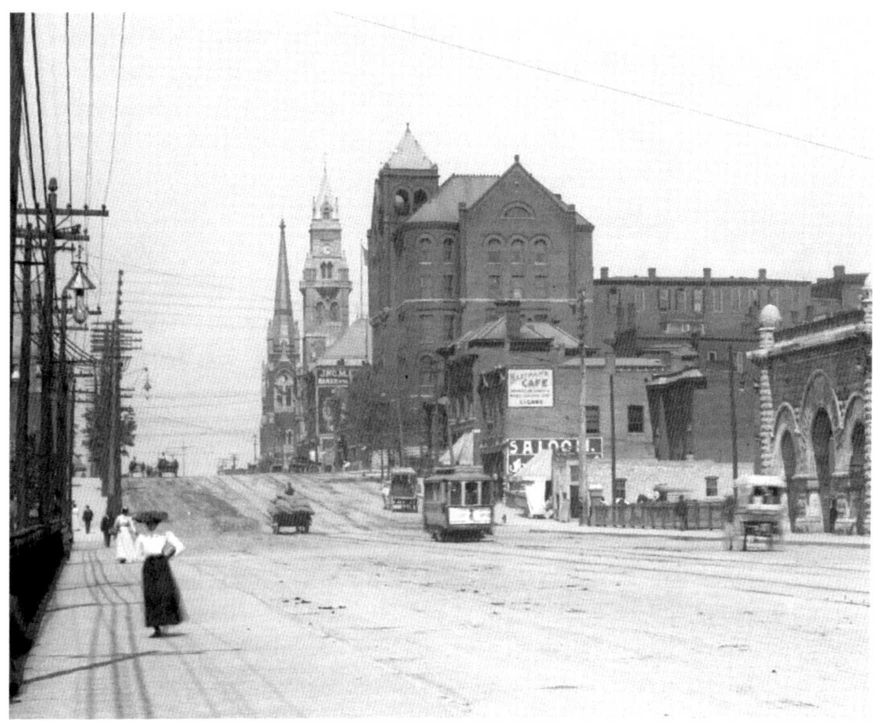

Broadway in 1900. The large dark building in the center is the Vauxhall Apartment building. The building housing Jackson's barbershop is just visible beneath the sign reading "Jno. M. Baker." It was here that one of the most startling murders in the city's history took place. *Enlargement of a Library of Congress photo.*

Unfortunately, we only have Anna Dotson's version of her final conversation with Charlie. As she told it, while Cobb clipped little Scott's locks, Anna whispered that she'd confessed everything to her husband and implied that he would be looking for the barber. They needed to end their relationship. His reaction was not what she expected.

Cobb, she said, was upset but not cowed. He said he was expecting it, and if they came at him, "he would not be caught napping." Anna decided that she had to act before her husband got into a shootout with her boyfriend.[86] However, nobody else overheard this crucial conversation. Witnesses said they spoke in an animated fashion but that neither looked angry or distressed.

When she got home that night, she grabbed the pistol that her husband had given her for self-protection when he was out of town and slipped it into her hand warmer. The rest was obvious. "I did not do it to revenge myself," she declared from behind the bars, "only to protect those that I love."[87]

The times, they were a-changing in 1913. On the very day Anna carried out her rash act, the headlines were shouting that the suffragettes were on the march in London and Washington, fighting for the right for women to be considered full citizens. Even so, it was still very much a Victorian, male-dominated society, where the local paper routinely ran a section titled "What Women Are Doing Worth Hearing About."[88] The idea of a female taking such a direct approach in a matter like this shocked the city's conservative sensibilities. Traditionally, women were supposed to turn to a male friend or relative to avenge them if they were "wronged" or "outraged." But in a case like this when two women were victimized and two families shattered by the same crime, the old tradition went out the window.

Charlie Cobb may have been a rogue, but his wife, Daisy, still loved him, and she and her child were left with nothing after his murder. She proved to be a formidable adversary, determined to prosecute her husband's killer to the full extent of the law. Cobb's heartbroken father came from his home in Big Rock to take his son's remains home for burial and testified at Anna's arraignment. As it turned out, the elder Cobb was a former sheriff of Stewart County, and with his connections as a lawman combined with his daughter-in-law's fierce desire for retribution, it was clear that this matter was not going to be swept under the rug. The scandal would be smeared all over the town by the time all was said and done.

As soon as the news broke, Dr. Dotson hired an attorney and drove to Nashville to be with his wife. Their reunion at the police station was powerful. As she was led from her cell, she walked toward him, white as a ghost and shaking all over. Without a word, she slid her arms around her neck and buried her face in his chest, sobbing. Dr. Dotson put his arms around her as well, and for several long moments the officers and attorneys stood by awkwardly, allowing the couple to have their tearful reconciliation. Within a short time, she was released on $5,000 bond and returned home to Gallatin in her husband's automobile.

The arraignment was a circus. If the couple was trying to avoid publicity, their worst nightmares were about to come true. Crowds of gawkers surrounded them on their way to court, including more than one hundred of their neighbors from Gallatin. Some were surreptitiously snapping photos as they went, prompting Dr. Dotson to call one a "dirty scoundrel!"[89] as his attorney smashed the shutterbug over the head with his cane, nearly breaking his camera.

Before the judge, Anna Dotson stood emotionless, her jaw set firmly as lawyer K.T. McConnico did the talking and pleaded not guilty on behalf of

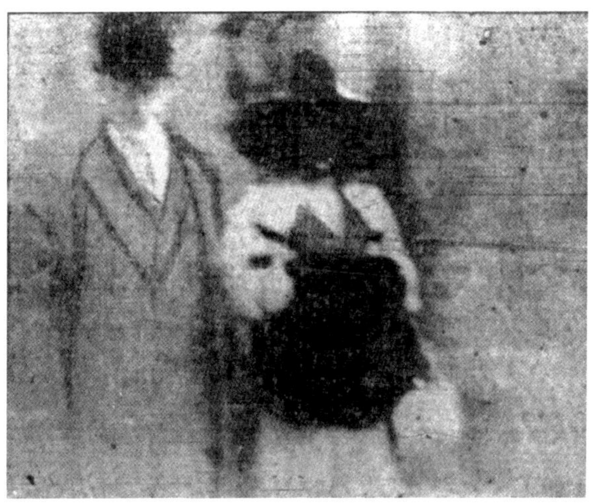

This remarkable photo shows the Dotsons leaving court after her arraignment for murder, still holding the muff that concealed her revolver. The poor quality is due to the fact that Mrs. Dotson's attorney clubbed the photographer with his cane as this shot was snapped. *Courtesy Tennessee State Library and Archives.*

his client. There was little doubt as to the outcome of the hearing—after all, she did blow a man away in broad daylight in front of half a dozen witnesses. As expected, the grand jury indicted her for first-degree murder and the judge increased her bond to $20,000. Bail was swiftly posted by several prominent citizens, and Anna and her husband went home to Gallatin on the same day's evening train to pass the next few weeks until her trial date.

It would come down to twelve jurors—all men—to decide the matter. Was Anna Dotson a wronged soul driven to the brink of madness by a seductive cad? Or was she a cold-blooded vamp who had not only used an innocent man for her amusement but also murdered him when he became an inconvenient obstacle to her future happiness? As can be imagined, the public flooded into the courtroom when the trial opened on June 16, 1913.

Daisy Cobb, dressed in deepest mourning with a heavy black veil over her face, testified first. When asked whether she knew the defendant, she locked eyes with Anna Dotson and coldly said, "I do." She went on to testify that they had been very close, often playing hide-and-seek in the yard with their kids. She had noticed Mrs. Dotson paying attention to Charlie but never anything improper. When asked, "Did you love your husband?" Daisy replied, "I did," and broke down. "And did he love you?" She could only nod through her sobbing.[90]

The defense put her through an hour and a half of grueling cross-examination, but Daisy Cobb held her own. She stepped down and spent the rest of the trial staring daggers at the woman who had killed her spouse. All in all, it was a powerful display of grace and righteous anger. The defense had an uphill battle.

It was standing room only in the hot, stuffy courthouse as Mrs. Dotson herself took the stand and gave her version of events. As could be expected, it was a rather one-sided affair, reiterating her claims that she'd striven to be good and only given into Cobb's advances once in July 1912 and never again. She presented herself as a woman betrayed by her own emotions and then wickedly manipulated by the barber, who used their conversations about religion to maneuver her into a compromising position.

However, the postcards and letters that passed between herself and her lover—helpfully provided by Daisy Cobb—seemed to indicate a much earlier and more frequent intimacy between the two. And she herself let a few choice admissions slip, such as, "I was interested in him….I fought against it and was surprised at myself." On one such occasion, she admitted her brother was asleep in another room, and she was asked why she didn't call out to him for help when—as she said—Cobb attempted to force himself on her. "Because she loved Cobb," she admitted, "and didn't want him and her brother to have any trouble."[91]

The preacher's daughter also said that, driven to desperation, she privately made what she called "Jephthah's vow" from the book of Judges: if the Lord delivered Charlie Cobb into her hands, she would gladly offer herself up as a sacrifice. Her family reverend testified that he knew of this "vow" and had tried in vain to get her to see it as foolish and not a proper Christian thing to do. He did admit that he was fully aware that she intended to kill her betrayer, and he was asked whether he'd done anything to try to stop her from going through with it. He said no.

The reverend was also asked whether he'd advised Anna that if she'd willingly accepted Cobb's attentions, she had acted wickedly; but if Cobb had forced himself on her, she was within her rights to shoot him. Interestingly, the man of the cloth dodged the question, replying that he'd never thought otherwise than Mrs. Dotson had been seduced. He never answered whether or not he'd planted the idea of killing her seducer.

The testimony got stranger from there. Astoundingly, given her original statements about her husband's anger, Anna now said she had begged Walter to kill her after confessing, that she wasn't worthy of living. "He said that he could not live without me," she testified. She also said that Walter had secured Cobb's Nashville address for her and that she had prayed to God to give her the strength to carry out her vow as she headed for the barbershop that day—somehow implying that both her husband and the Almighty were accomplices after the fact. She claimed she'd taken the dress she wore when she first met Cobb and used it for target practice, asking her husband afterward if "bullets would prove fatal if fired into a body at those places."[92] The implication was that Dr. Dotson knew beforehand what she was up to but never moved to stop her from carrying out her vow. It was a bizarre performance, to say the least. Far from her initial statement that she had killed Cobb to keep her husband out of it, it now seemed she was implying that the shooting might have been Walter's idea and he had used her as an assassin to bump off his rival.

The prosecution then asked her about her last conversation with Cobb the day before the shooting. Was it not true, they inquired, that she'd actually gone to Jackson's in a desperate attempt to get the barber to take her back and run away with her? Her reaction was rather interesting. Turning white with rage, Mrs. Dotson hissed, "Anybody that says that is a lie!"[93]

Perhaps realizing that their client sounded more than a bit off during her testimony, the defense brought out "alienists" who specialized in mental abnormalities to testify that Mrs. Cobb was temporarily insane and unable to tell right from wrong at the time she shot her lover. She was, they testified, "for the time being, a monomaniac."[94] In other words, her religious upbringing had deluded her into thinking divine providence had provided the means for her to kill Cobb. As they began their testimony, Mrs. Cobb, who had been resting her head on her arms wearily, suddenly sat bolt upright and began to stare intently at the proceedings. The prosecution team attempted to derail them in cross-examination, but unfortunately, they were out of their depth when it came to psychological matters, and the experts stuck to their guns.

It was a grinding weeklong ordeal. As the proceedings wrapped up, Anna sat pale and nervous with her husband and children behind her attorneys. A short distance away, Daisy Cobb, poised and determined in her widow's weeds, took a seat with her daughter and father-in-law as the final act began.

It was now for those twelve men to decide, and both sides played heavily on the traditional notions of womanhood. Mrs. Dotson, the prosecution maintained, was a murderess of the worst kind. "The female of the species was more deadly than the male," they said, as "the male usually gave some outward sign of…anger, while the female…smiled on the victim as she sent a bullet through his heart."[95] But the defense came back with prose most purple about "the seducer" who came "with his deceptions and lies, worming himself into the midst of the family and causing the woman's downfall," comparing the wreckage of her life and home to a tornado that had recently laid waste to part of the city, while paying "a glowing tribute to womanhood," leaving many of the men in the jury box wiping the tears from their eyes.[96] As an added touch, a group of suffragists stood around Mrs. Dotson during this recitation, weeping in solidarity with the defendant.

It was late in the afternoon when the jury members received their instructions and retired to deliberate. They were out for twenty-one hours, but at two o'clock on the afternoon of June 24, 1913, they filed back into the courtroom to render their findings. "A dead hush overspread the crowd that packed the room," one breathless reporter said, noting that when the jury room door opened, Anna Dotson "became deathly pale."[97]

In the hush that followed, the judge asked if they had reached their decision. They had, and the foreman gave their verdict: guilty of involuntary manslaughter. Then they pronounced the sentence.

Five days to be served in the county workhouse.

If the legal minds gathered that day looked "thunderstruck," it was for good reason. To this day, Anna's sentence stands as the lightest ever given for homicide in a Nashville courtroom.

As the crowd murmured and the defense team congratulated themselves, Judge A.B. Neil thundered that he was extremely disappointed in the outcome, saying that the jury's finding was no less than a "miscarriage of justice." Some observers openly wondered if the fact that Dr. Dotson and most of the jurors were brother Masons had something to do with it. Red-faced, Judge Neil announced that he was disappointed in the verdict, adding rather lamely that "she shall serve every minute of it!"[98] The defense team smiled and announced that they had no objection, and Mrs. Dotson was taken into custody by the jailer, saying farewell to her husband and children.

As the verdict was read, Daisy Cobb stared in shock and then collapsed forward, head in hands, completely defeated. A reporter asked her opinion, and she wearily responded, "Of course I am disappointed, but I don't care to say anything else."[99]

Anna Dotson would serve her sentence, but it certainly wasn't hard time. She was driven to the workhouse on First Avenue. Since she was the "only white woman" in the institution, she was housed at the assistant superintendent's residence.[100] The next day, clad in a plain calico dress, she went to work sweeping the floors and scrubbing dishes for the work crews breaking rocks on the roads for the county. In fairness, the work was tedious, and she was given no privileges, but it was a light penance in the minds of most.

At 5:00 a.m. on June 28, Dr. Dotson pulled up in front of the "county Bastille," and his wife, clad in an outfit "more befitting her station in life," stepped into the car for the drive back to Gallatin. She cut a check for $54.80

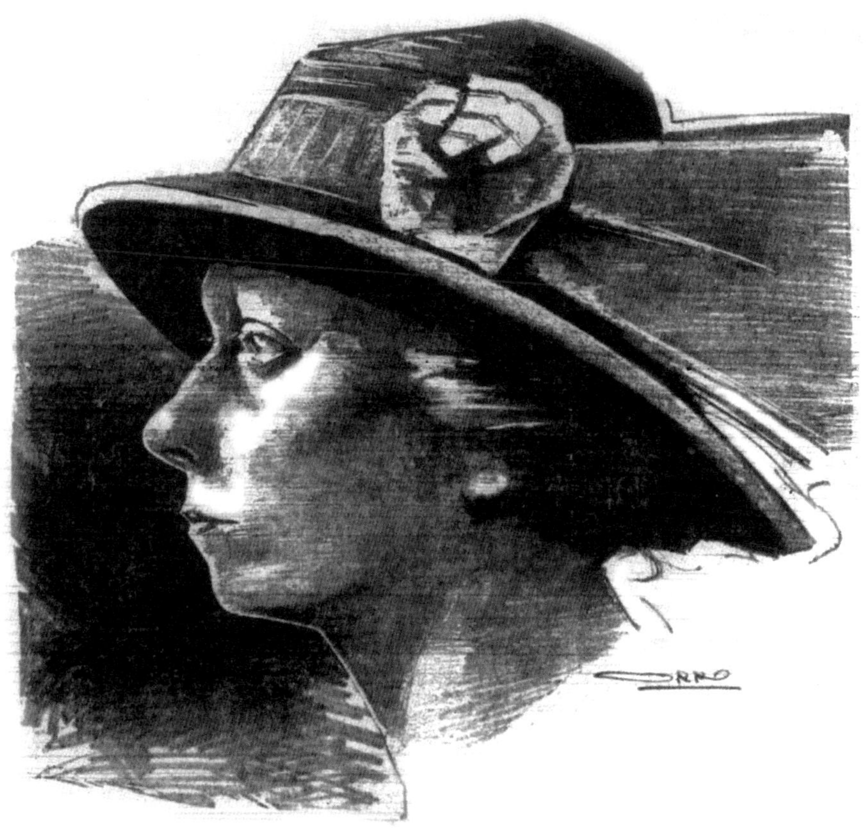

The camera-shy Anna Dotson was sketched by a newspaper artist surreptitiously as she sat in court listening to the testimony that would decide her fate. *Courtesy Tennessee State Library and Archives.*

to cover the costs of the prosecution, and that was the end of the matter. She disappeared back into the respectable obscurity she and her husband so desired. Despite her professed monomania, the couple lived a peaceful life together. Dr. Dotson quietly continued his practice until his death on March 13, 1926, at the age of only forty-eight. Anna followed him on July 21, 1948, and was buried next to him in the Gallatin City Cemetery. She was sixty-eight.

Daisy Cobb faded into the ether as well, moving on with her own shattered life, and gradually the sensation died away, leaving as many questions as answers. It's hard to say whether justice was truly done. Cobb was doubtlessly guilty of seducing Mrs. Dotson, but given her own testimony, it's hard to believe that she was entirely unwilling. In hindsight, the tragedy seems a natural result of a society with one foot in modern times and the rest of its body in the past. In so many ways, the Dotson affair was the city's first twentieth-century "sensation" trial, but at heart, it reflected dying Victorian sensibilities, some of which still linger a century later.

A remarkably prescient comment was made in an editorial letter that was published just as the trial was winding up. S.A. Craig wrote in to express his wonder at the double standard of society. When Mrs. Dotson confessed to her husband, he asked why Dr. Dotson did not feel equally compelled to confess his own missteps to her. "Why is it that women are held to so much stricter observance of the moral and sacred laws of chastity than men? I believe that men should be held to the same…requirements along this line as women, and should suffer precisely the same penalties."

"I remember a case of this kind that was brought before Christ," Craig continued. "Some men brought a woman to Him, charged with…adultery, and Christ asked them what was their verdict. They replied: 'To be stoned to death.' Then the Saviour said: 'He among you who has not sinned, cast the first stone.'"[101] One wonders what the preacher's daughter thought of his example. The point was valid: if it hadn't been for the pressures of society, would she have felt compelled to kill in order to salvage her public reputation? Would she have been judged the same if she were in Cobb's place? But as it was, Anna felt compelled to cast stones despite her own sins. And somehow Daisy Cobb, the only one who seems blameless in all this, ended up suffering for everyone else's misdeeds. Society remained remarkably silent about *her* ordeal.

It's a struggle that continues down to today. Certainly, the bullets fired that day in Jackson's barbershop weren't the first such stones ever cast. And sadly, they wouldn't be the last.

CHAPTER 9

PUBLIC ENEMIES

Ask around town and you might hear all sorts of legends about Nashville playing host to some big-name criminals at some time or other. One of the most enduring is that Al Capone himself used to frequent the city during the palmier days of Prohibition.

The stories are legion: Al used to run Tennessee moonshine direct from Nashville to Chicago. He used to come down to meet with a high-ranking associate in town. He had a hideout or gambling hall on the outskirts of town. Some folks even claim to know the address.

Unfortunately, there are few facts backing up these stories, and none of them makes logical sense. As much as it may gall some locals, Nashville was small potatoes in the 1920s, and if Capone had any business in the area, it would be very unlikely he ever came here to oversee it personally. He had guys on the payroll to handle things like that, and if there was a problem…well, you went to him, not the other way around. About the only time Capone is known to have come to the city was in 1931 after his conviction for tax evasion when the train taking him to the Atlanta Federal Penitentiary stopped over at Union Station and gave the locals a thrill as they snapped photos of the big-shot gangster through the window glass of his railroad car.

So if Al Capone had so little to do with the place, why all the stories? Author Elizabeth Goetsch has an intriguing theory that suggests people are confusing their gangsters. It's possible that when people tell stories about Capone, they're really thinking of another legendary figure, a near contemporary of the Chicago crime lord. And unlike Al, this one really did spend some time in the city.

John Herbert Dillinger was just as famous as Capone in his day. He wasn't a syndicate gangster but rather a professional bank robber who came to prominence knocking over "jugs" across the Midwest. He had a penchant for automatic weapons and fast hot rods and a wisecracking mouth that made him the darling of the press.

His career was incredibly short and violent, spanning just one year, and most of his robberies were staged in Indiana, Ohio, Illinois and Minnesota. But on at least two occasions, he and his gang visited Nashville, leaving some colorful local legends in their wake.

Dillinger himself was only here once, and his stay was unremarkable. After killing a cop in Chicago in December 1933, the gang needed to lay low for a while, so they drove south to Nashville, where they planned to catch a train for Florida. Dillinger, as "Frank Sullivan," registered at the posh Hermitage Hotel along with his girlfriend, Billie Frechette. They were joined there by gang members Harry "Pete" Pierpont, Russell "Booby" Clark and John "Red" Hamilton, along with their lady friends. They stayed a couple of days, during which Pierpont went to a jewelry store on Union Street where he purchased a silver watch for his companion, Mary Kinder. Then they boarded a train at Union Station bound for Daytona Beach, where they spent the Christmas holidays.

At the time of his visit, Dillinger was a wanted man, but what happened afterward would make him a criminal legend. After Daytona, the gang headed for the backwater desert town of Tucson, where they planned to hide out for a while. Unfortunately for them, the local police were sharper than they suspected, and the entire gang was picked up without a shot being fired. Pierpont would later be tried and convicted of the murder of an Ohio sheriff and went to the electric chair in October 1934.

Dillinger was extradited to Indiana to stand trial for murder and placed in the maximum-security jail at Crown Point. Somehow, he managed to get hold of a carved wooden pistol, and on March 3, 1934, he used it to bluff his way out of custody. The sheer audacity he displayed, rightly or wrongly, made him a folk hero overnight. Within weeks, he was holed up in St. Paul, Minnesota, where he began actively organizing a new mob.

Among his colleagues were two very tough customers. John Hamilton, thirty-four, known as "Red" after his hair color, was originally from Ontario but grew up in Indiana. His nickname "Three Finger Jack" was a testament to his steely nerve. He earned it when he took a bet as a child to see how

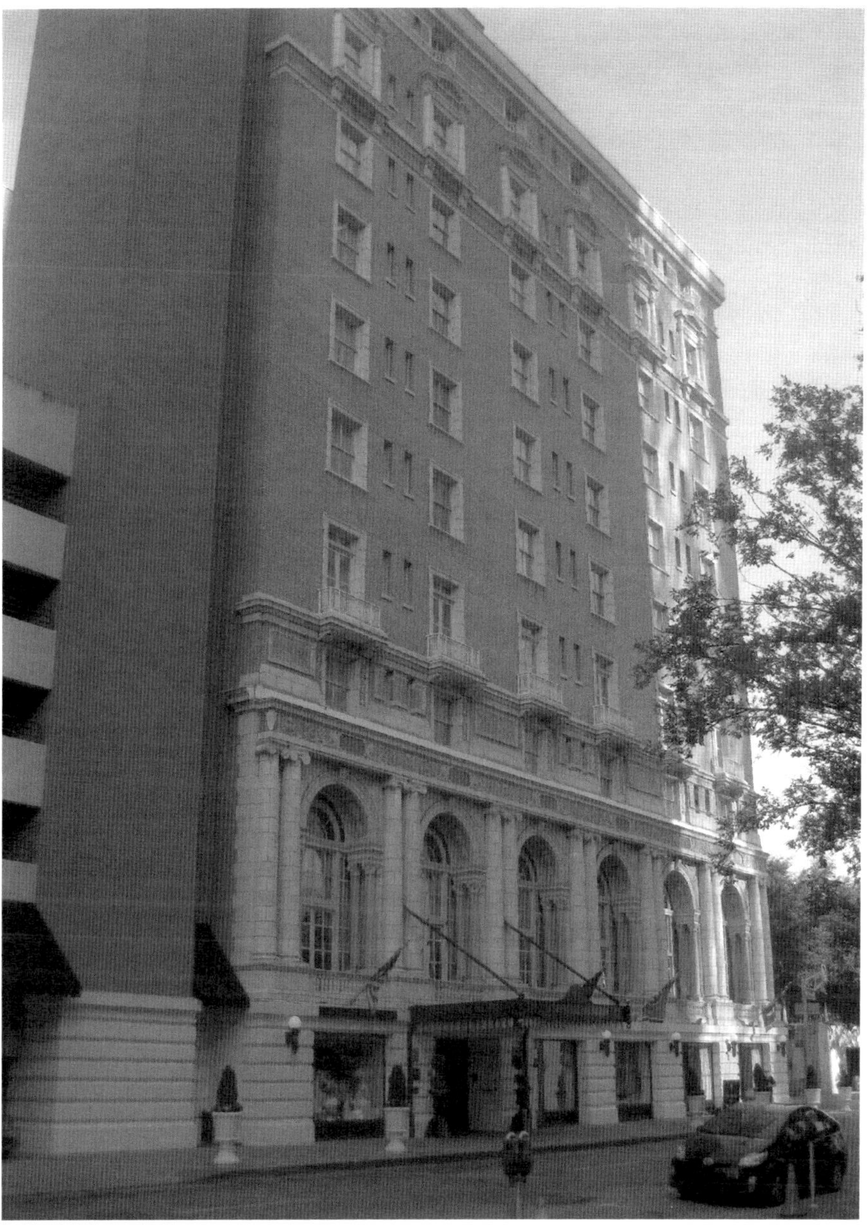

The Hermitage Hotel, Sixth Avenue. In December 1933, John Dillinger and several partners in crime stayed here under assumed names. *Author's photograph.*

close he could steer his sled to a moving railroad train. He won but came so close to the wheels that he had to put his right hand out to keep from going under, and the train removed two of his fingers. The loss of his digits didn't seem to affect his shooting skills though, and he had already killed one policeman and had been wounded several times in shootouts. Hamilton had been a member of the original gang and had stayed at the Hermitage with Dillinger on their first visit the previous year. Tough, cool and quiet, he was probably Dillinger's closest friend and ally.

Homer Van Meter, on the other hand, was an interesting contradiction in human nature. In today's parlance, he "didn't have a filter," and it's quite possible that his behavior stemmed from a genuine mental aberration. Sleepy-eyed and homely looking, he had a crude, immature sense of humor and was given to slapstick and practical jokes. He seemed to wander through life completely oblivious of the danger he was in or the trouble he caused others. The clown of the gang, he nevertheless had a very dark side and was a ruthless killer, responsible for the murder of no fewer than three cops by the time all was said and done. But for all his goofiness and his quick temper, Van Meter had an uncannily quick wit and was a master of bluffing his way out of trouble through sheer brass.

He showed this trait well on the afternoon of March 30, 1934. The police raided the apartment in St. Paul where Dillinger and Billie were living as "Mr. and Mrs. Carl Hellman." The cops were unsure of what they were dealing with, and when Billie stalled them by saying she wasn't dressed, they patiently waited while Dillinger armed himself inside. As this standoff was going on, Homer wandered right into the midst of everything. The officers quickly asked him who he was.

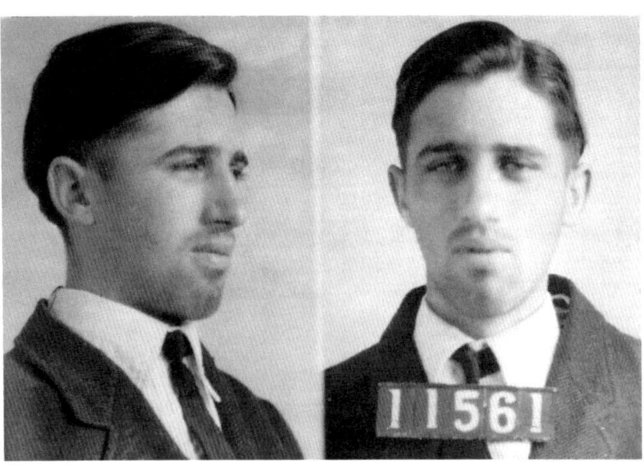

Homer Van Meter, a gunman who seemed to attract trouble wherever he went. *Indiana Images Collection, DG-019, Indiana State Archives.*

With his crooked smile, Van Meter handed them an unbelievably ludicrous line: "I'm a soap salesman."

Incredibly, they bought it, and an FBI agent accompanied him downstairs to his car where he said he had proper identification. Once they were out of sight of the other officer, Van Meter pulled a .45 automatic and growled, "You asked for it, so I'll give it to you!" He chased the agent across the front of the building while emptying a clip at him but didn't manage to hit anything. Just then, Dillinger opened fire from his apartment with a submachine gun, spraying chunks of plaster and blasting a way out. He was hit in the leg, but he and Billie managed to get away clean. Thankfully, the cops were unhurt, though embarrassed.

Meanwhile, Van Meter ducked into a side street, hijacked a horse-drawn delivery wagon and used it to make a fittingly bizarre getaway, cramming the driver's cap down on his head as he lashed the horses into a gallop. Despite this reliance on nineteenth-century technology, he was able to ditch the police and get away scot free.

While Dillinger holed up in a safehouse in Minneapolis to heal, Van Meter hunted up Red Hamilton and went into hiding. Shortly afterward, someone tipped the cops off to their own hideout, so they decided to get out of the area until the heat blew over. At the time, heading to Tennessee seemed like a stroke of genius—after all, who would be looking for them there? In fact, it proved to be a miscalculation that soon landed them in hot water.

Accompanied by Pat Cherrington, Hamilton's vivacious redhaired girlfriend, the pair of gangsters drove east from St. Paul on April 2. The next known sighting of them came at 9:00 p.m. on April 9, when they checked in at the Crow's Nest Tourist Court in Kingston Springs, twenty-four miles west

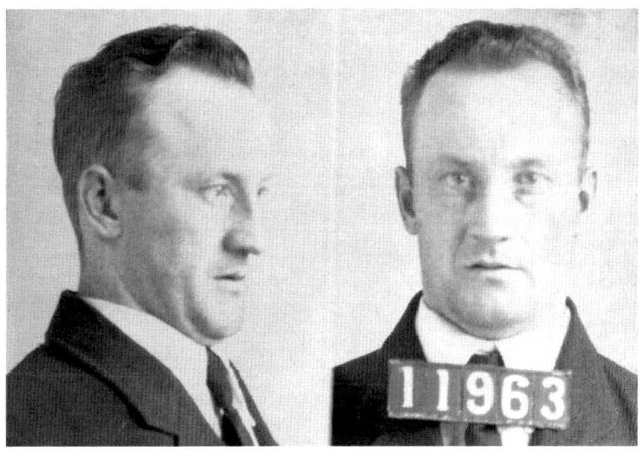

John Hamilton, one of Dillinger's oldest and closest friends. *Indiana Images Collection, DG-012, Indiana State Archives.*

of downtown Nashville. They registered as "Mr. and Mrs. Oswald Jennings and Brother" from Knoxville, and they attracted little attention among the usual crowd of tourists—although the manager of the Crow's Nest did notice one oddity. He said the three ordered steaks for breakfast from the café the next morning and that one of the men asked the redheaded woman in the party to cut up his meat for him, "as though some trouble existed with his hand."[102] It seems that Hamilton (who had dyed his distinctive hair black) couldn't outrun his childhood accident.

Still, they caused no trouble, and no alarms went off. They took a secluded cabin surrounded by a clump of trees, well back from the main road. It should have been an ideal hideout, but without ears on the ground they had no idea they were stepping into a hornet's nest—for once not of their making.

Nashville was on edge that spring due to its own homegrown crime wave. The Depression spawned larceny throughout the country, and a wave of violent robberies by local youths, including the notorious Blue Sedan Gang, meant the police were out in force watching local businesses carefully. Strangers were bound to attract notice, and the three midwestern gangsters didn't exactly blend into the local scene.

After breakfast on the tenth, the trio drove over to Murfreesboro, where they pulled up to the Rutherford County clerk's office in a black Ford V-8 sedan at about 9:00 a.m. Pat Cherrington went inside, where she instantly drew unwanted attention from the deputy clerk, Mrs. J.O. Abernathy, who just didn't like her looks. Mrs. Abernathy described her as "stockily built… well but not flashily dressed." Cherrington said she wished to purchase a license for her husband who had just bought a used car.[103] The clerk thought something was off about her customer and carefully studied her appearance, noting that her red hair was dyed and her hands were stained by cigarettes.

The woman gave her name as Mrs. Harmon L. Osgood and said she was staying at the James K. Polk Hotel. She was relaxed and unhurried, making polite chitchat as she filled out the paperwork and paid the necessary fees before walking out with license number 176-103. As soon as the mystery woman left, Mrs. Abernathy called the hotel, which said that nobody by that name or description was registered. She also put in a call to the sheriff's office, but by the time that officer showed up, no trace of the woman could be found.

Later that night, around 9:30 p.m., the outlaws stopped into the Southern Café, where they ordered country ham and eggs. Proprietor Jimmy Haynes said the woman seemed nervous and he thought she'd been drinking, and he said that Van Meter kept getting up and leaving the table during the meal. He thought they were acting strangely and watched them closely, making small talk with Hamilton, who said they were on their way to Chattanooga. He later identified his mysterious visitors from a group of mug shots, saying, "I made a close study of their faces and cannot be mistaken."[104] In fact, he was: somehow he had mistakenly identified Van Meter as John Dillinger himself.

They spent most of April 11 driving in and out of their campground on various errands. Around sundown, Van Meter and Hamilton drove into Nashville to buy supplies. At around 10:30 p.m., they pulled into the parking lot of Walker's Drugstore on West End Avenue. They had picked up a local contact in town, as three men were in the car at the time. This third man has never been identified.

At the time of their visit, business owners were on edge because of the wave of recent holdups, and the store employees had noticed a shifty-looking group of kids hanging around near the door. Van Meter was behind the wheel and spotted the same group. With a professional's eye, he suspected that they were planning a robbery, and he reacted in typical fashion—for him. He ordered cherry Cokes brought out to the car and then sat back to watch the kids knock the place over.

As they sat there sipping their drinks waiting for the floor show, they didn't notice as another car pulled into the lot carrying two plainclothes Nashville policemen. Normally, Officer T. Vernon was a motorcycle cop and John Byrd was a patrolman, but because of the crime wave the pair had been put on extra duty in an unmarked vehicle, looking for suspicious activity. Something about the three men in the Ford seemed to warrant extra investigation, so the rotund Byrd stepped out of their patrol car and walked quietly up to the driver's side window.

"Do you live in Nashville?" he asked, taking Van Meter by surprise. However, the gangster reacted with his typical presence of mind. Without missing a beat, he casually replied, "No, I live in Knoxville. Why?"[105]

"I'm an officer of the law," Byrd said before being rudely interrupted by something poking him in the ribs from the sedan's rear window. He turned—and found himself staring down the barrel of a fully loaded Thompson submachine gun in the hands of John Hamilton. In a "clipped Northern twang," Hamilton calmly but firmly ordered him to "Get the hell back in your car, and drive toward town."[106]

Caught flatfooted, Byrd backed up slowly as Hamilton pointed the Tommy gun at his midsection and repeated his order twice more. Vernon

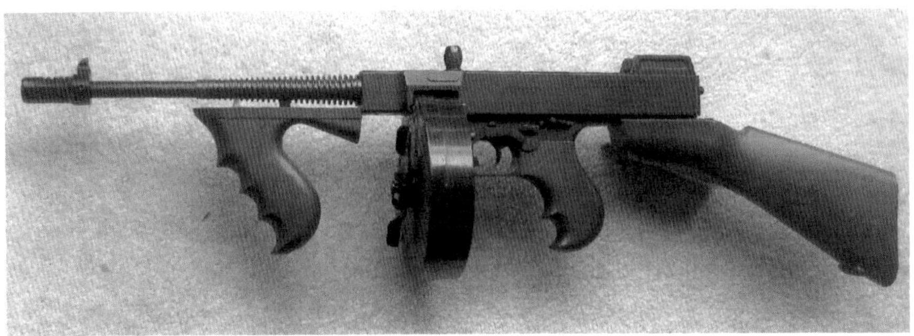

The Thompson submachine gun was favored by outlaws and lawmen alike. This weapon would claim an unexpected victim during the hunt for the gangsters. *Author's photograph.*

was caught behind the wheel of the patrol car, and neither of the officers felt like committing suicide by going for their own guns while faced with an automatic weapon. Vernon leaned across the front seat and shouted for his partner to get back in the car. Byrd backed up and stumbled, landing on his rear end on the car's running board. Scrambling back up, he finally managed to claw the door open.

The moment he did so, Van Meter put the Ford in gear and stomped the accelerator, lurching back down the Harding Pike, the brake lights disappearing behind a cloud of dust. It wasn't their finest hour, but at least the cops did manage to get the license plate: Tennessee 176-003. It was the same plate Pat Cherrington had purchased the day before in Murfreesboro.

In the confusion, the kids who had been casing the joint slipped away, leaving one with the sneaking suspicion that this marked the only time the Dillinger mob actually saved a business from being robbed, albeit accidentally.

Back at the tourist court, Pat had a feeling something was wrong. John and Van had been gone much longer than she expected, so from instinct born of long experience she began packing their bags—just in case. Soon afterward, the black Ford pulled into the Crow's Nest at top speed, going so fast that Van Meter drove past their cabin and had to back up a bit. As the boys got out of the car, they met Pat coming out of the cabin with their things. Hurriedly, Hamilton explained that they'd been "jumped up" by the local law and helped her throw the bags in the car.[107] By midnight, they were tearing through the Tennessee countryside on their way out of the state.

There was much slapstick attached to their escapades in Nashville, but unfortunately the entire affair would end with a tragedy. As the word went out that Dillinger's crew was in town, the police called in every available man to join the search. Among them was William G. Ezell, a fifty-year-old deputy sheriff, who reported to the Davidson County Jail where a search party was organizing.

Detective Leo Flair was holding the butt end of a Thompson submachine gun when Ezell grabbed a fifty-round drum magazine and attempted to load the weapon. Somehow, he ended up standing directly in front of the muzzle as he fumbled to get the magazine locked into place. Just as Flair warned, "Be careful," the bolt slipped, and the gun went off, firing one round that struck Ezell in the left side of the chest and tore through his abdomen, exiting from the right side. He was bundled into a car and rushed to St. Thomas Hospital, where surgery was performed, but to no avail. He died four days later. Inadvertently, the gang had managed to take the life of another lawman, though Ezell is not generally counted with the thirteen other victims of their crime spree. A popular farmer and family man, he was buried at Woodlawn Cemetery with an honor guard of policemen escorting him to the grave. He was survived by his wife and two sons.

In the end, the best efforts of the local police came to naught. Using the back roads, the gangsters got away clean and were back on home turf in time to join Dillinger in a raid on a police station at Warsaw, Indiana, three days later. Their luck couldn't last forever though, and the FBI dragnet was closing in. Their future could be measured in weeks.

Dillinger himself went down on the evening of July 22, 1934, shot down in Chicago by FBI bullets after being put on the spot by Anna Sage, the legendary "woman in red." Homer Van Meter went out in almost identical fashion a month and a day later. On August 23, he was sold out by his underworld connections and cornered by police in a blind alley in St. Paul. He went down in a gutter shredded by twenty-five slugs, dead at the age of twenty-eight.

Patricia Cherrington was convicted of harboring federal fugitives and spent two years in prison. By the time she was released in 1936, she was seriously ill from a failing gallbladder. She spent her final years scraping out a bleak existence as a waitress and died in Chicago from her health issues in 1949 when she was forty-five.

The most mysterious fate was reserved for Red Hamilton. According to the official version, Hamilton was shot in the back during a police ambush in Minnesota on April 23, just two weeks after leaving Tennessee. He was taken to an underworld doctor in Chicago, but due to the extreme heat on the gang, nobody would treat his wounds, and he soon developed gangrene. He died at a safehouse in Aurora, Illinois, a week after being shot and was

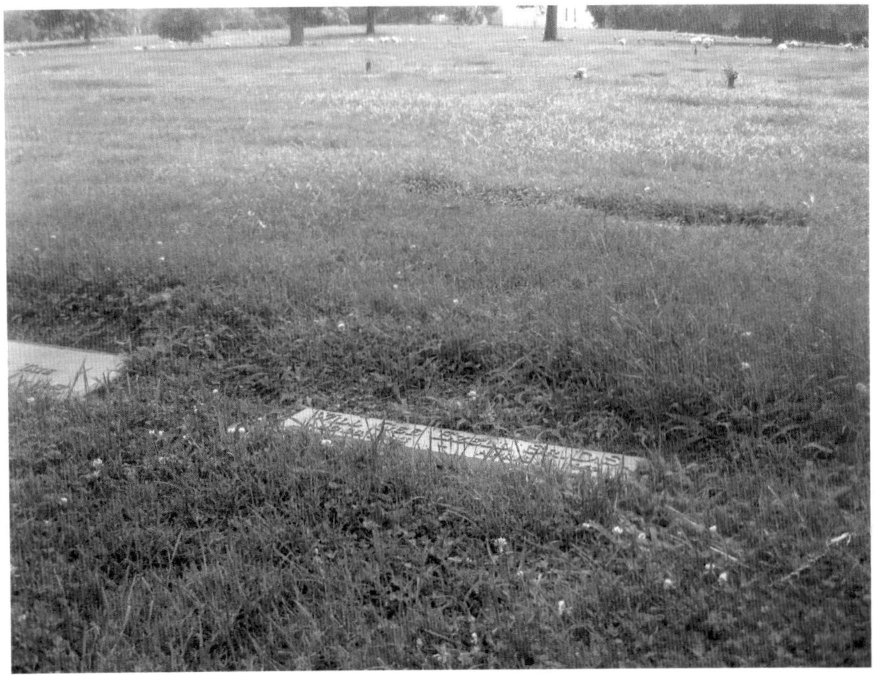

Deputy Will G. Ezell's grave at Woodlawn Cemetery. *Author's photograph.*

secretly buried in a gravel pit outside Oswego. According to an informant, Homer Van Meter and "Ma" Barker's son Doc were the grave diggers, and John Dillinger gave the eulogy. "Red, old pal," he said, "I hate to do this, but I know you'd do the same for me," before he dumped a can of lye on Hamilton's face to obscure his features.[108] Underworld tipsters later informed the FBI, who had the remains disinterred the following year and identified them using prison dental records. If the story is accurate, Red Hamilton would have been thirty-five.

There is a more romantic version, though. According to this story, Hamilton ended up the only member of the gang to cheat justice. One of his nephews recalled a family trip to Michigan in 1946 when he met a relative he'd never seen before. He was afterward told that he had met his uncle John Hamilton, very much alive more than a decade after his supposed demise. He claimed that Red later moved home to his native Ontario, where he died quietly in the 1970s, outliving his old nemesis J. Edgar Hoover.

It's a colorful legend, and similar tales have been told of other famous outlaws, from Billy the Kid to John Dillinger himself. Unfortunately, no hard evidence has ever surfaced to back up these stories, and without it they remain just that—stories. Unless more proof turns up, the most likely scenario is that Red Hamilton died a miserable and painful death on a cot in a cheap apartment rented by fellow hoods.

Unlike Chicago, New York, St. Louis or Detroit, Nashville never had a real "gangster era," but on this one memorable occasion at least it played host to some of the most colorful villains in American history. At the same time, as we shall soon see, the city had its own troubles stemming from a parcel of homegrown outlaws who, while not as well known, were every bit as vicious as the "big boys" from out of state.

CHAPTER 10

THE DIRTY '30S

During the Depression, America seemed besieged by criminals. Bank robbers, kidnappers and mobsters roamed the countryside, and colorful thugs like "Pretty Boy" Floyd and "Baby Face" Nelson appeared daily in the newspapers and over the airwaves, terrifying and thrilling the public at the same time. While gangsters like Floyd and Nelson were wholesale offenders operating over wide swaths of territory, Nashville's criminals were strictly retail, confining their operations to the city and the surrounding countryside. In the spring of 1934, one such group of local bandits launched an ambitious robbery spree that ultimately resulted in several deaths. Reckless and bloodthirsty, they would be remembered as Nashville's own small-time version of the Dillinger mob. They became notorious in the press as the Blue Sedan Gang.

The leader of the bunch was Rufus R. Guy, one of the rough-and-tumble sons of Rodney and Hattie Guy who always seemed to be on the bad news side of things. Born on December 10, 1908, Rufus was one of seven children and grew up drifting from place to place as his father sought work. At various times they lived in Hopkinsville, Kentucky, and Springfield, Tennessee, before settling in East Nashville around 1930. By that time, Rufus was employed as a cooper in a barrel factory—at least during the day. By night, he and his younger brothers were getting up to no good. Their nocturnal escapades finally landed them in trouble.

In July 1931, Rufus and several companions broke into the store of W. Phillips on Stewart's Ferry Pike. They were surprised as they were leaving by

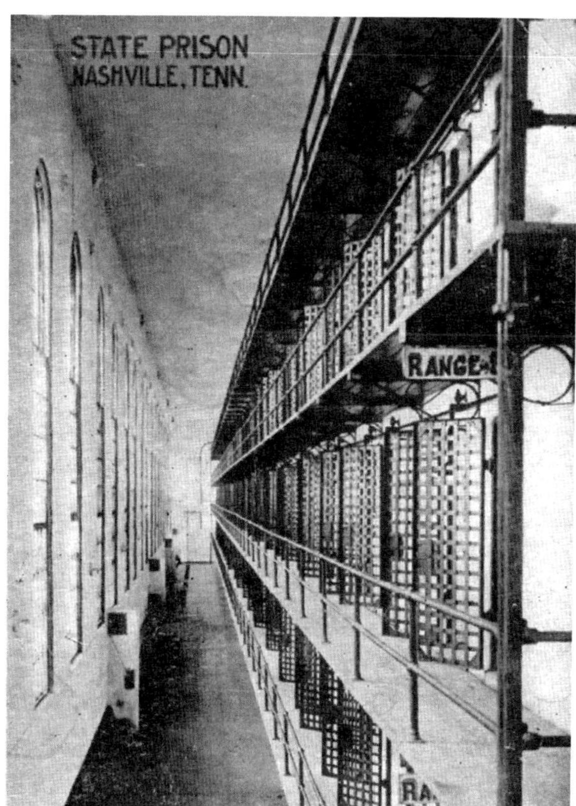

A cellblock in the Tennessee State Prison around 1900. Things looked little different thirty years later when Rufus Guy was an inmate here. *Author's collection.*

Josh Perry, an African American watchman, who opened fire on them. The group returned fire, wounding Perry as they hightailed it from the scene. Later that morning, they were jumped near Murfreesboro Pike by Detective Leo Flair, who ordered them to put up their hands. Guy responded by raising his shotgun and pulling the trigger, but the weapon misfired, and no harm was done. The bandits escaped through a field, and for several months nothing was heard from them.

On October 15, the police knocked at Guy's parents' door on Howerton Avenue, and when he tried to run out the back way he was tackled and wrestled to the floor by four detectives. He was charged with housebreaking and grand larceny, and because he had snapped his shotgun at Detective Flair, they threw in assault with intent to murder for good measure. While waiting for his trial, he made no friends among the authorities when he joined an attempt to break jail led by cop killer Horace Woodruff. Five prisoners jumped and slashed a trustee, but the attempt failed when the trustee decked Woodruff and slammed the door on the conspirators.

Guy was convicted at trial the following month and sentenced to three years in the Tennessee State Prison. He was twenty-four years old, with blue eyes and brown hair, and on his arm was a "Tattooed Heart with dagger thru [*sic*] it."[109] His education was listed as fourth grade level.

Prison life was rough. Conditions were primitive and nasty, and beatings were frequent and arbitrary. He later recalled, "Back then, you either had to work, or you got the leather strap."[110] Despite this, he managed to keep his nose clean and accrued a year of credit from his sentence. He was paroled on November 17, 1933, just two years after he went inside. Like many who went through the experience, he came out a much more hardened and dangerous man than when he went in.

He wasn't alone among his siblings. His kid brother Lawrence was convicted of housebreaking in 1930. Too young for prison, he was sent to the juvenile detention facility at Jordonia. On the evening of November 15, 1931, he broke out, firing three shots at a pursuing guard as he disappeared into the surrounding brush. His parents were accused of providing the gun—the first firearm ever used in a breakout from that place. His freedom proved short-lived, and he was soon recaptured and brought back. Lawrence never achieved the notoriety of the others. He spent the next decade in and out of trouble before finally being shot dead by his own wife in 1940.

Then brother Earl was convicted of robbery on October 13, 1932, and sent to the State Prison the same day to start a five-year sentence. He proved as impatient as his brother, and on January 22, 1934, he simply walked off a work detail at the truck farm. His escape marked the birth of a new gang whose rampage would be long remembered in Nashville.

After breaking out, Earl looked up his brothers Rufus and Eldon. The three reunited Guys formed the core of the new outfit, and they recruited other tough kids from their neighborhood like Tommy Scalf and Philip Rimlinger. They got hold of a small arsenal of pistols and shotguns. Then they needed some wheels.

On the evening of February 28, 1934, they spotted the perfect vehicle: a new blue two-door Ford V-8 sedan, license number 195-188, parked near the intersection of Twelfth Avenue and Broadway. They promptly swiped it, and the distinctive automobile would almost act as a trademark for them in the weeks to come.

Unlike some of the bigger-named gangs of the era, the Guys were strictly small time. They avoided big risks like banks and concentrated on nickel-and-dime scores, hitting small stores or sticking up lone targets and taking them for pocket money. However, they offset this by the sheer number of the jobs they pulled and were easily some of the most prolific robbers in the city's history.

Their method was brazen and reckless. In their first three days in action, from March 1 to 3, the gang pulled no fewer than seventeen robberies, speeding from one score to the next while the police scrambled to catch up. The night of the third was particularly hectic. They began by driving out to Goodlettsville, where they held up a store, and then turned the sedan back to Nashville on Dickerson Pike before doubling back again. By the time they arrived back at Goodlettsville, reports of the blue car had preceded them, and the stores had all locked their doors to keep the robbers out. Frustrated, they turned toward Nashville once more, one step ahead of the law.

At 7:45 p.m., they pulled up next to a pedestrian crossing the Bordeaux Bridge on Hyde's Ferry Pike and ordered him to "fork over" his money. At eight o'clock, they pulled up in front of a drugstore on Twenty-Third Avenue North. Three men got out while one kept the car running. After getting $105 from the register, they walked into the neighboring barbershop and took $12 more before getting back in the car and roaring off.

Shortly afterward they hit a grocery store run by a man named Perdue, but the proprietor was no pushover. The bandits pulled guns and ordered him to put up his hands along with the other six people present. Perdue defiantly kept his hands firmly in his pockets as Rufus Guy stuck an automatic pistol under his nose and said, "If you don't stick up your hands, I'll blow your damned brains out!"

Stubbornly, the grocer still refused, and a second gangster yelled, "Lay him down! Don't fool with him!" Guy grabbed him and pulled him forward, firing the gun at the same moment. The bullet grazed Perdue's hip and bounced off a stovepipe, knocking him to the floor. They fled the scene thirty-five dollars richer, but almost immediately a police car spotted them and gave chase. A few miles down the road, they ditched the pursuit and escaped. Luckily, Perdue was not badly wounded in the incident.

So it continued throughout the night, always the same. The car sped up, three men ran in spouting death threats and waving weapons and then ran out again with whatever they could grab. By ten o'clock, they were roaring back out of the city with every policeman in the district on their trail. Incredibly, they pulled one more job in Goodlettsville before knocking off for the night—their seventh of the evening. In all, their three days' work had netted them more than $1,300.

The community was up in arms. It had been a spectacular display of lawlessness on a scale that even cities like Chicago rarely dealt with. Due to the telltale getaway vehicle, the press swiftly dubbed the quartet the Blue Sedan Gang, and the police immediately put every available man on the case. The men were small timers, obviously, but what worried them was the sheer volume of activity and the suspects' reckless use of firearms. Nobody could wave guns around like that without someone getting killed sooner or later. It turned out to be sooner.

Around eight o'clock on the night of March 7, Carl Patterson, a cabbie driving car no. 88 for the Yellow Cab Company, pulled into the cab stand in front of the Hermitage Hotel on Sixth Avenue, where he picked up a fare. The passenger, described as a tall, thin youngster with a "pimply face," dressed in dark clothes, told Patterson to drive him into the countryside.[111]

About thirty minutes later, they were bumping down the mud-rutted White's Creek Pike when they came to a spot where the backwaters from the Cumberland were blocking the road. At that point Patterson announced he could go no farther and turned the cab around, so the passenger said he'd get out there. Patterson walked around to open the door but found that the other man was holding a .32-caliber revolver in his hand.

"Give me your money," the bandit said. "I might as well take it here as any other place." Patterson, desperate in the hard times of the Depression, had only a small amount in his pocket. As he later told a policeman, "I had to save that $12. It was all I had."[112] He began yelling for help, and with that, the robber opened fire. Patterson was shot in the arm, the bullet entering his armpit and passing through the lungs, and then a second one entered his side, perforating his intestines. Despite that, the wounded cabbie grabbed a jack handle and tried to brain the shooter as he jumped from the cab. The gunman escaped into a field while Patterson staggered to a nearby residence, where an ambulance was called. He was taken to General Hospital, where he was able to give a description of his assailant before he died the following day. Only thirty-eight years old, he was survived by his parents, a daughter and several siblings. He was buried in his family's cemetery at Caney Springs.

Amazingly, Patterson's replacement was held up a month later while driving no. 88, leading fellow cabbies to conclude the vehicle was jinxed. Unlike Patterson, the other driver wasn't hurt.

Now that murder had been committed, the police faced even greater pressure to stop the crime wave. Complicating their job was the fact that the Blue Sedan bunch wasn't the only gang operating in the city at that time. In addition to various lone bandits, a three-man outfit from out of town was also robbing stores and service stations in the area. This bunch also pulled a more ambitious job, knocking over the Western Union office in the

Stahlman Building on March 11. The police were stretched thin dealing with all the chaos.

Incredibly, the Blue Sedan Gang's reign of terror lasted only three weeks, during which time they were suspected of dozens of holdups. They eventually ditched the telltale blue sedan, but their final night in action started much the same as the others. At around 9:30 p.m. on March 17, two men got into a cab at the corner of Fourth Avenue and Church Street and gave the driver an address on Eighteenth Avenue North, where they pulled pistols and forced him out of the driver's seat. They drove the stolen cab out to their usual stomping grounds on White's Creek Pike, where they robbed the cabbie of eleven dollars before driving away, one of the pair taking their victim's cap for good measure.

The robbers then held up a family traveling in a yellow roadster, robbing them and taking the car as well, then proceeded out the Clarksville Pike to Paradise Ridge. As they topped remote Germantown Hill, they saw the headlights of another car coming toward them and turned the stolen vehicle so as to block the road.

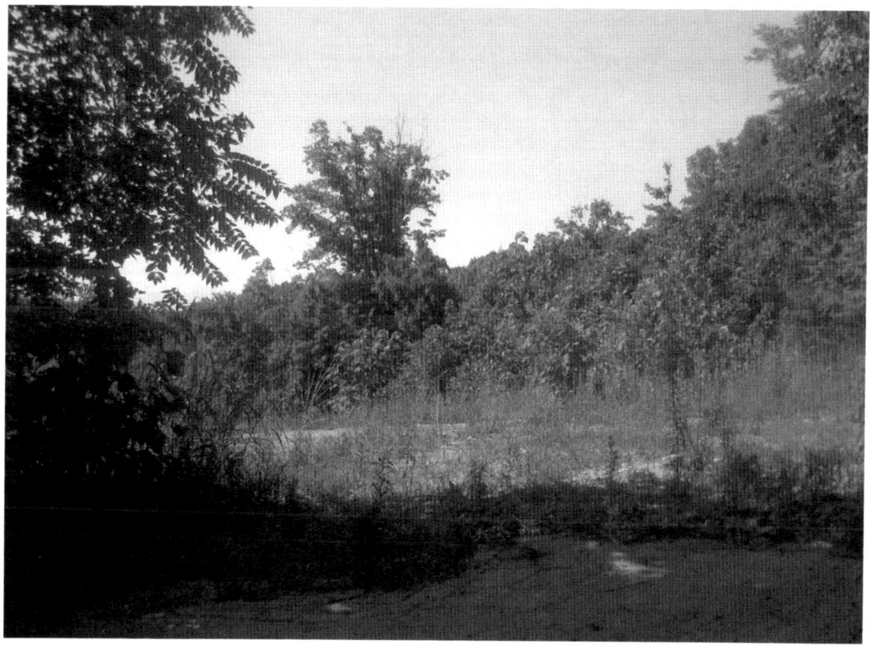

A recent shot of Germantown Hill on Paradise Ridge. It was near this spot that Charlie Sanders had his violent confrontation with the Blue Sedan Gang. *Author's photograph.*

They had no idea that the other car was driven by a policeman. Officer Charlie Sanders, fifty, was off duty that night and had agreed to drive his friend Mrs. E.T. Knox to visit some mutual acquaintances north of town. Sanders took it all in at a glance, and when the yellow car spun out and several men jumped out of it, he knew it had to be a holdup.

He pulled his .38 service revolver and told his companion, "Duck down. I'm going to shoot it out with them."[113] As the lead bandit jumped on the running board, Sanders fired twice through the open window into his face. The man jerked and dropped to the dusty road, a .32 revolver flying from his hand. Sanders then emptied his weapon at the others before slamming his car into gear and gunning around back down the road in a swirl of dust. The other bandits opened fire, one peppering the door and windshield of his car with a sawed-off shotgun. Luckily, the pellets did no damage. The other bandit emptied a .32 automatic at the fleeing vehicle's tail lights.

A short distance down the road, Sanders began to slump behind the wheel. Mrs. Knox asked, "Are you hit?" He murmured, "Yes, in the stomach." After a short distance he couldn't hold the wheel steady any longer, so Mrs. Knox slid into the driver's seat and took over, driving at breakneck speed to the residence of Henry Hackbiel. The bandit car chased them a short distance, but Mrs. Knox shook them and soon arrived at the Hackbiels' gate, where she called for help.

Unfortunately, it was too late. Charlie Sanders was already dead. An autopsy determined that one of the .32 pistol slugs had hit him in the shoulder, severing the subclavian artery. He died within minutes.

The Blue Sedan Gang were now cop killers, and the entire police force turned out to bring them in, dead or alive. They only had one clue, but it turned out to be all they needed. They had the body of a dead bandit.

Sanders's victim turned out to be Earl Guy, the twenty-five-year-old escaped inmate. He'd been struck in the neck and the temple by shots from the officer's pistol. It didn't take a genius to figure out who his accomplices might have been. An army of twenty-five cops swarmed the Guy family home at 416 Brannon Street early the next morning and took Rufus and Eldon Guy without firing a shot, along with the boys' father, Rodney, who was charged with aiding and abetting. A search of the home showed how lucky the lawmen had been. Not only did they uncover a small arsenal of pistols and the shotgun used in the shootout, but they also found a dugout under one room where the floorboards had been sawed away. It's safe to say that had the brothers not been surprised, they could have made the house into a fortress and withstood a long siege from within.

The police fanned out and soon had Tommy Scalf and Philip Rimlinger in custody as well. By coincidence, the three gangsters from the Western Union holdup were arrested in Detroit the same day and extradited to Tennessee to face charges. Overnight, two dangerous gangs had been taken out of circulation. Charges against Rodney and Eldon Guy were later dropped, but evidence recovered from the family home was enough to charge the other suspects with multiple counts of robbery, as well as the murder of Officer Sanders. Ballistics also determined that slugs from the slain Earl Guy's pistol had killed cab driver Carl Patterson three weeks earlier, solving that crime as well.

In custody, the gangsters quickly turned on one another. Scalf and Guy readily confessed to the holdups but denied killing Sanders. They tried to pin it on Rimlinger, both of them saying he'd fired the shotgun that night. Evidently they were under the mistaken impression that buckshot had killed the officer. Rimlinger denied it heatedly and tried to deny he was even in the car when the shootout occurred. According to their version of events, after Earl was shot and killed, Scalf stood up in their stolen roadster's rumble seat and emptied his pistol at Sanders's car, while Rimlinger fired the shotgun and Rufus fired two rounds from his pistol as well. Based on their confessions and an FBI ballistics report, it appears that the fatal shot actually came from one of Scalf's bullets.

The trial was swift and merciless. The jury was out for only eight minutes before returning with a guilty verdict, and the trio barely avoided a date with the electric chair. The sentence was harsh enough: ninety-nine years for each. They were sent to the State Prison the same day to begin their terms.

The world they entered was harsh and primitive. "Ten Pen," as the convicts called it, was a dank, nasty throwback to the nineteenth century where filthy conditions, harsh punishments and sudden death were all facts of life. The '30s were an especially low point in the institution's history, and their time inside would take its toll on all of them.

Philip Rimlinger would never see the outside again. In 1949, ailing and repentant, he made a bid to have his sentence reduced to life so as to be eligible for parole but was turned down flat. He died on September 5, 1959, at the age of fifty-one.

It was only at his parole hearing that it emerged for the first time that Tom Scalf had already been paroled, a move that raised eyebrows in many places. Scalf had been far from an ideal prisoner and had gotten into several scrapes with other inmates. In 1939, he had stabbed fellow inmate Charles Mayor to death in the prison tuberculosis hospital in an argument over a newspaper.

However, the good time that he lost for the killing was later reinstated, as Mayor was seen as the aggressor in that incident. Despite Scalf's poor behavior, Governor McCord signed a secret parole for him on January 14, 1949. When asked for comment, Officer Sanders's son was outraged. The younger Sanders had joined the police department after his father's killing and was adamant that he would have appeared before the parole board to protest had he known about the move. Why Scalf walked was never explained, though there was speculation that he was either seriously ill or had turned informer while inside.

That left Rufus Guy, the roughest of the lot. His story was destined to be the most colorful of the lot as well.

Guy went in angry and remained that way. In March 1938, he escaped but was swiftly recaptured. Then that November, he threw in with several of the most desperate men in the prison, staging a spectacular breakout that ended in a furious gunfight with authorities. Guy was riddled with buckshot and nearly killed during the incident, and worse yet, Assistant Warden C.C. Woods was mortally wounded. Guy and the others nearly landed in the electric chair. They would have burned except that Woods lived just a little over a year, which was the legal limit for a murder charge. Nonetheless, Guy and the others spent much of their time on the "White Line" in solitary confinement for their role in the escape.

Yet time has a way of declawing even the fiercest old lions. During the '50s, a new reform movement was introduced into the prison, and even tough old cons like Guy were given new freedoms and a chance to prove themselves trustworthy. After several failed attempts, he won his parole in 1965 and was released into a much different world than the one he'd left thirty years before.

It was the era of Vietnam and Watergate, with a new cynicism to go with it. The world of his youth was being romanticized on screen as two similar small-time Texas punks named Bonnie and Clyde were suddenly transformed into counterculture antiheroes. On the radio, a mustachioed singer named Jim Croce was crooning a tune about a "Hard Time Losin' Man."

One wonders if Guy ever heard it. He certainly could have related.

Freedom was not kind to the old bandit. In 1970, when he was sixty-two, the Shelbyville police came to his house to arrest him on three warrants for armed robbery in Alabama. They ended up shooting him in the hand and the right leg, which was later amputated at the hospital. He would spend three years in prison in Alabama before being paroled back to Tennessee.

Upon his return, he found himself in the unusual role of crime victim. While living at a halfway house he befriended Earl Skaggs, who'd done time in Tennessee for armed robbery. He considered the young man a friend and at one point lent him $40 to help him make rent. On November 16, 1974, Skaggs and a partner picked up Guy at the facility and drove him out to Joelton, where they stopped alongside White's Creek Pike at a spot known locally as "Devil's Elbow." There, they dragged Guy out of the car and robbed him of $400 before beating him half to death with his own crutches. One of them cut Guy's throat, but before he could finish the job, they were interrupted by a police cruiser. The two suspects fled but were immediately run down by a K-9 unit, and Guy was taken to Baptist Hospital in critical condition. Miraculously, he survived.

Ironically, the scene where Guy's life nearly ended was only about two miles from where Charles Sanders had been gunned down almost exactly forty years before.

He emerged from the hospital a broken, washed-up man, but ironically the prison he'd once called home wasn't done with him yet. Sometime in

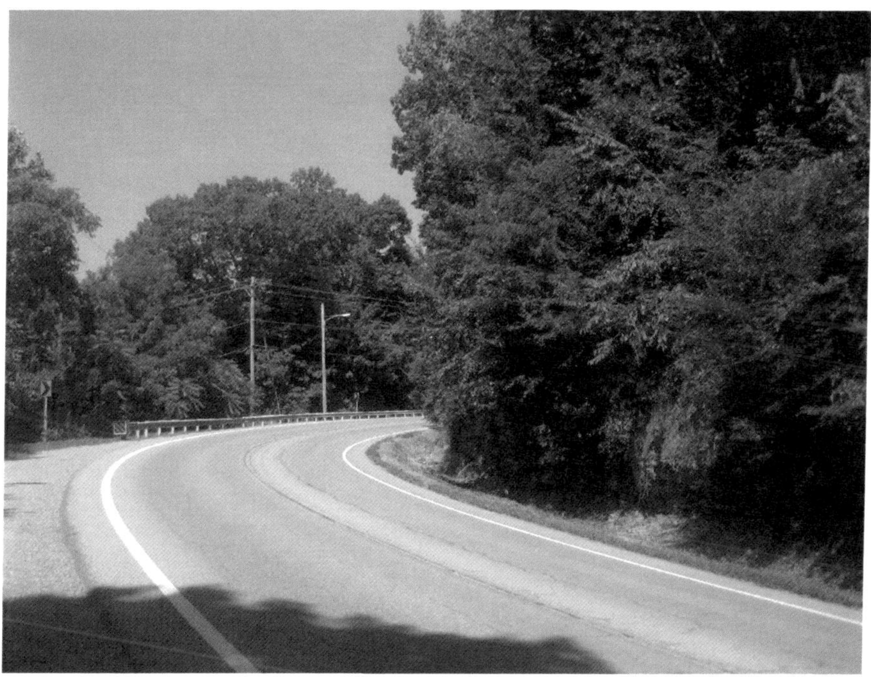

The infamous "Devil's Elbow" near Joelton was only a few miles from where Sanders was slain. Ironically, former gangster Rufus Guy was robbed and nearly killed here twenty-nine years later. *Author's photograph.*

1977, he was arrested in Shelbyville once more for parole violation—he got drunk and out of hand, and his landlord called the police. At sixty-nine years of age, he found himself back behind bars once more in the Tennessee State Prison. Stooped, toothless, tottering on his crutches, he made a pathetic figure.

Compared to his early years in the joint, he found conditions markedly improved. "Prison is 100% better today," he told a reporter, saying it was "just like a big, old reformatory." Still, he wished he was anywhere else. "I wish I hadn't gotten into this trouble because it's a rough way to spend your life." He went before the parole board a few days before Christmas 1977, asking them to let him leave in time for the holidays. His prospects were stark; a few relatives still lived nearby, but he had no wife and no children and nowhere to go when he got out. Still, he pleaded for their sympathy, saying, "I don't want to die in this place."[114]

He had to spend Christmas inside, but eventually the parole board granted his wish, and on February 6, 1978, he limped out of the gate a free man, never to return to the gray stone walls that had been so much a part of his life. He had four more years to live, passing away in 1982 at his home in Shelbyville.

With him passed an era—not a particularly glamorous, era as is sometimes shown in the movies, but a desolate time of hardship and grinding poverty. The Blue Sedan Gang were tied to their times, a product of the Great Depression and all its desperation. Although sometimes we like to look back on that time as a quaint and simpler era, the truth is that those days were closer to our own than we like to think. And it was an era that would forever leave an ugly mark on the soul of the city.

CHAPTER II

UNSPEAKABLE

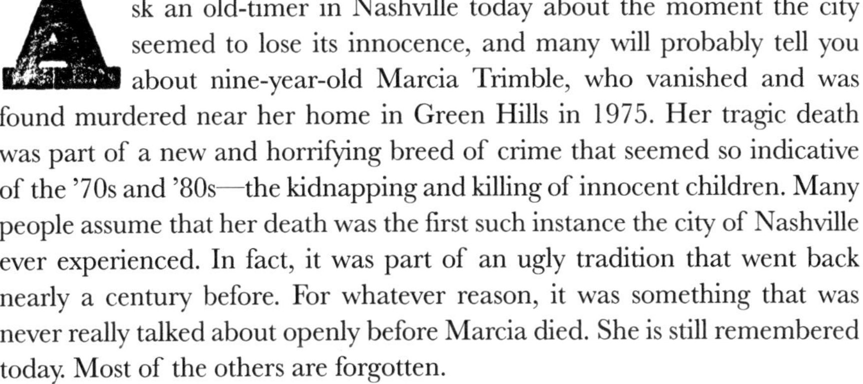

Ask an old-timer in Nashville today about the moment the city seemed to lose its innocence, and many will probably tell you about nine-year-old Marcia Trimble, who vanished and was found murdered near her home in Green Hills in 1975. Her tragic death was part of a new and horrifying breed of crime that seemed so indicative of the '70s and '80s—the kidnapping and killing of innocent children. Many people assume that her death was the first such instance the city of Nashville ever experienced. In fact, it was part of an ugly tradition that went back nearly a century before. For whatever reason, it was something that was never really talked about openly before Marcia died. She is still remembered today. Most of the others are forgotten.

The first time it happened was all the way back in October 1884, when twelve-year-old Jimmy Raymer disappeared near the home of his father, a saloonkeeper on First Street. Days later, he was found beaten to death in a culvert along the L&N Railroad just over a mile from his home. As far as is known, nobody was ever prosecuted for the boy's death. Given that he was delivering a large sum of money for his father at the time he died, it seems that his death may have been a robbery attempt gone wrong.

While rare, children did occasionally fall afoul of monsters even during the "good old days." It was well into the twentieth century before authorities fully realized that these crimes weren't just aberrations—that there really were people sick enough to target the innocent. For Nashville, that realization actually came forty-one years before Marcia Trimble disappeared. The story begins in a quiet neighborhood on September 19, 1934.

Around 1:15 p.m., the kindergarten run by Mrs. David Rice at 113 Scott Avenue let out for the day, and the seventeen children in attendance started for their homes. Among them was six-year-old Dorothy Ann Distelhurst, whose father, Alfred, worked as an "estimator" for the Methodist Publishing House.

Strange as it seems today, despite her young age, "Dottie" often walked the six blocks to her parents' house unescorted, as did many of the other children. Minutes after she left the school, she was seen on a sidewalk near the railroad crossing on Scott Avenue by a classmate, six-year-old Marcella Chamberlin, who was home sick that day. She was standing on the porch of her house and watched Dottie pass by, dressed in a blue-and-white dress with a bundle of schoolbooks and a pink lunchbox dangling from her hand. "She waved at me,"[115] Marcella recalled. At that point in her walk, Dottie would have been about halfway home. It turned out to be the last time Dorothy Distelhurst would be seen alive.

By suppertime, it was quite clear that something was wrong. Dottie had never arrived at her home, and as night fell, her parents became increasingly anxious and began looking for her. By 6:00 p.m., Mr. Distelhurst approached his neighbor, Constable Frank Stull, and told him that his daughter was missing. Stull wasted no time contacting both city and county police, and within hours, a full-scale search was underway. A perimeter of six square miles was established from Eastland Avenue to Cahal, and volunteers began beating the brush. In a scene that has since become chillingly familiar, they walked shoulder to shoulder, tramping through overgrown lots and yards, calling out Dorothy's name as their flashlights and lanterns stabbed into the darkness.

Neighbors went door to door recruiting their friends. Eventually, over four hundred people were combing the neighborhood, aided by the headlights of automobiles lined up on the streets to illuminate the scene. Vacant buildings, tool sheds and outbuildings were thoroughly searched, but no sign was found of the little girl. The searchers toiled on for the next few days, dripping sweat in the late summer heat.

Police followed up on other theories. They quickly dismissed a tale that a strange car had been seen careening through the neighborhood just about the time Dottie vanished. They contacted local hospitals, thinking that perhaps she'd been struck by an auto and taken in for medical care by a stranger. They also got in touch with the L&N and inspected the trains that

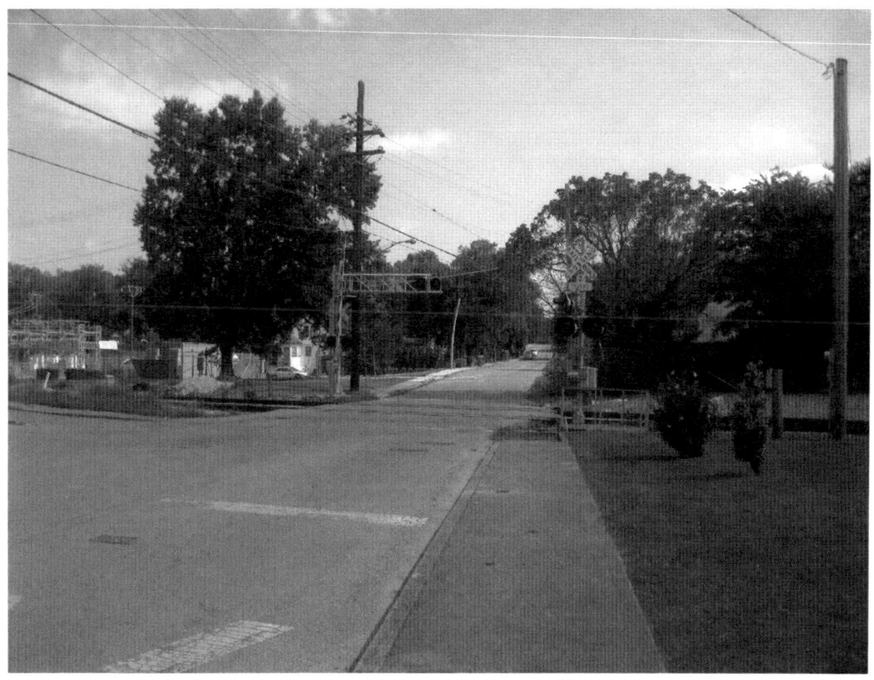

A 2018 photograph of the railroad crossing on Scott Avenue, eighty-four years after the crime. It was here that little Dorothy was last seen by a classmate walking home from school. *Author's photograph.*

had passed by that afternoon on the odd chance that the girl had been struck and tangled up in the mechanism of a locomotive. Neither hunch paid off.

They searched Martin's Hill, a "spooky" place shunned by neighborhood kids. It was a wooded knoll crowned by an old stone house whose last owner had committed suicide years before. The hill and house were both clean. There was just no sign of Dorothy anywhere.

As the search dragged on, the family understandably became more frantic. The press reported heartbreaking scenes from the house on Scott Avenue. Her father sat for hours in his study, afraid to leave his phone in case someone called with a tip or a ransom demand. Outside, the family's devoted German shepherd, Prince, paced nervously, dragging his chain across the yard, whining plaintively as he sensed the humans' distress. Dottie's younger sister, Martha Jean, refused to eat or play in the places she normally shared with her sibling. She slept fitfully and woke crying, asking her heartbroken nurse, "Why don't Dottie come home?" It was a question that the entire city was asking.

Strange developments soon came trickling in. Bloodstains were discovered on an overgrown trail that cut across a lot on Straightway Avenue just a block and a half away from the Distelhurst home. The blood was confirmed as human, though it couldn't be definitively linked to the missing girl. Nearby, a bloodstained man's handkerchief was found bearing the monogram "D." None of the Distelhursts recognized it.

The family began to suspect that their daughter had been kidnapped, a notion reinforced by the daily headlines covering the ongoing saga in New Jersey where Charles Lindbergh's baby boy had been snatched and murdered by ransom-seekers. While Alfred Distelhurst was no Lindbergh, he was comfortable enough that the notion of a ransom demand was not out of the question, and sure enough, a postcard soon arrived stating that further instructions were coming. The FBI stepped in to advise, but Distelhurst told the police to back out and leave a channel open so as not to spook any suspects. He communicated through the papers, telling the kidnappers, "Please contact me in any way you choose. The way is open."[116]

Meanwhile, the police were forming their own opinions. While nobody wanted to say it to the family, one of the hundreds of gawkers across the street dared to say it out loud. Pointing to a pigeon circling the dovecote on the family's garage, an old woman asked, "You know what 'at is? Why, 'at's the soul of that little girl, comin' back!"[117]

Inside, Mr. Distelhurst was racking his brain for answers. In desperation, he suspected that perhaps his wayward eighteen-year-old son, Alfred Jr., might have something to do with it, though he couldn't say why, beyond the possibility that the young man had bragged to the wrong guy about his father's money. He had stormed out of the house after an argument the previous November, and nobody knew where he'd gone. After six weeks of searching, the boy was finally located at a homeless camp near Jacksonville, Florida, and reunited with his family. However, there was no evidence at all that he'd had anything to do with his half sister's disappearance.

Dottie was a bright girl, remembered by her teachers as responsible for her age. Recently, she had taken the most difficult part in a class play. She had a sunny disposition and a brilliant smile, her family said, and she had been coached not to talk to strangers. She was also naturally bashful, which made her parents doubt she was led away willingly.

The Tennessee National Guard joined the search, sending three hundred troops to join the hundreds of volunteers combing the neighborhood. The headlines were full of depressing news: a convicted kidnapper was picked up in Kingsport, Tennessee, while chasing a child. Though he admitted

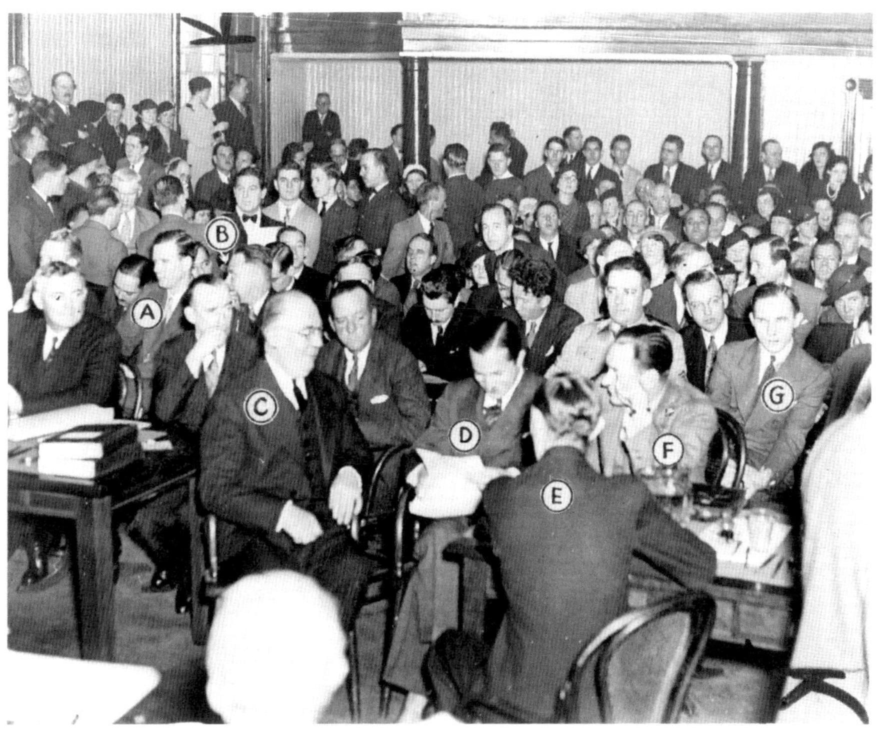

At the same time the tragedy unfolded in Nashville, an even more infamous one was occurring in New Jersey. In this photo, Charles Lindbergh (A) sits in the courtroom across from Bruno Hauptmann (G), who was eventually executed for the kidnapping and murder of Lindbergh's son. *Library of Congress.*

being in Nashville on the day of Dorothy's disappearance, he was never tied to the crime. In Detroit, Lillian Galliher, age eleven, was found dead in a trunk after being kidnapped near her home. And then there was Lindbergh. It seemed that the entire country was besieged by an army of predators attacking children. Incredible as it seems, Dorothy's disappearance wasn't even the first one on her street: Anna Mai Jones, a six-year-old neighbor, had disappeared earlier that summer, only to reappear in her own room so dazed she couldn't explain what had happened. Some theorized that her kidnappers had mistaken her for Dorothy and grabbed her, only to return the child when they realized the ransom wouldn't be as great.

Dorothy's disappearance was thought to be part of what was then called the "snatch racket," or kidnap for monetary gain. At the time, it was thought the only reason a child would be taken was for ransom, and sure enough, Distelhurst received a ransom demand for $150,000 from someone in New

York, instructing him to travel to that city to make the payoff. After some time, the demand was lowered to $5,000, and on November 10, Distelhurst left Nashville prepared to pay the kidnappers for the return of his daughter. While he followed the kidnappers' instructions, the FBI shadowed him, hoping to trail the gang. Sadly for all of them, the cloak-and-dagger business was nothing but a wild goose chase. As was about to become devastatingly clear, he had been the victim of a cruel hoax.

On the morning of November 13, two handymen on the grounds of the Davidson County Tuberculosis Hospital began digging some new flower beds at the northeastern boundary of the property near White's Creek Pike. They burned off some Johnson grass to clear the brush, and that's when one of the men noticed a small foot sticking out of the dirt. They raised the alarm, and a group of workers returned and unearthed the body of a small child.

She was found a few feet from the Hamilton Road bridge across White's Creek, face down in a cardboard box, covered with just two inches of dirt. Her clothes and personal belongings were found buried nearby. She had been quite obviously murdered. Her killer had gagged her and then struck her with a blunt object, probably a pole-climbing spike or an iron gate hinge, both of which were found nearby covered in blood. The blow was enough to shatter her skull, and she struck some other object as she fell, which fractured the bone on the opposite side of her head. Her face and shoulders were bare of flesh, leading to the conclusion that the killer had poured acid or lye over her face to destroy her features. She had probably been killed soon after her abduction; evidence on the body indicated that she'd been kept in the box that served as her coffin for several weeks before she was actually buried.

The news arrived in New York just as Alfred Distelhurst was preparing for the safe return of his daughter. He initially held out hope that the body wasn't Dorothy's, but the autopsy soon confirmed what everyone had feared. The heartbroken father boarded a rickety airliner at Newark Airport for the long flight back to Nashville.

The entire city was shocked by the little girl's death. Dorothy's funeral was held at Belmont Methodist Church, and she was buried in the family plot at Woodlawn Cemetery. Ruby Distelhurst collapsed, sobbing, as the flower-covered casket descended into the grave and had to be assisted back to the car by her family. Mercifully, the morbid curiosity seekers steered clear of the ceremonies.

Meanwhile, the investigation into her murder continued, but it was an uphill fight. The ransom notes were examined, and a striking detail emerged.

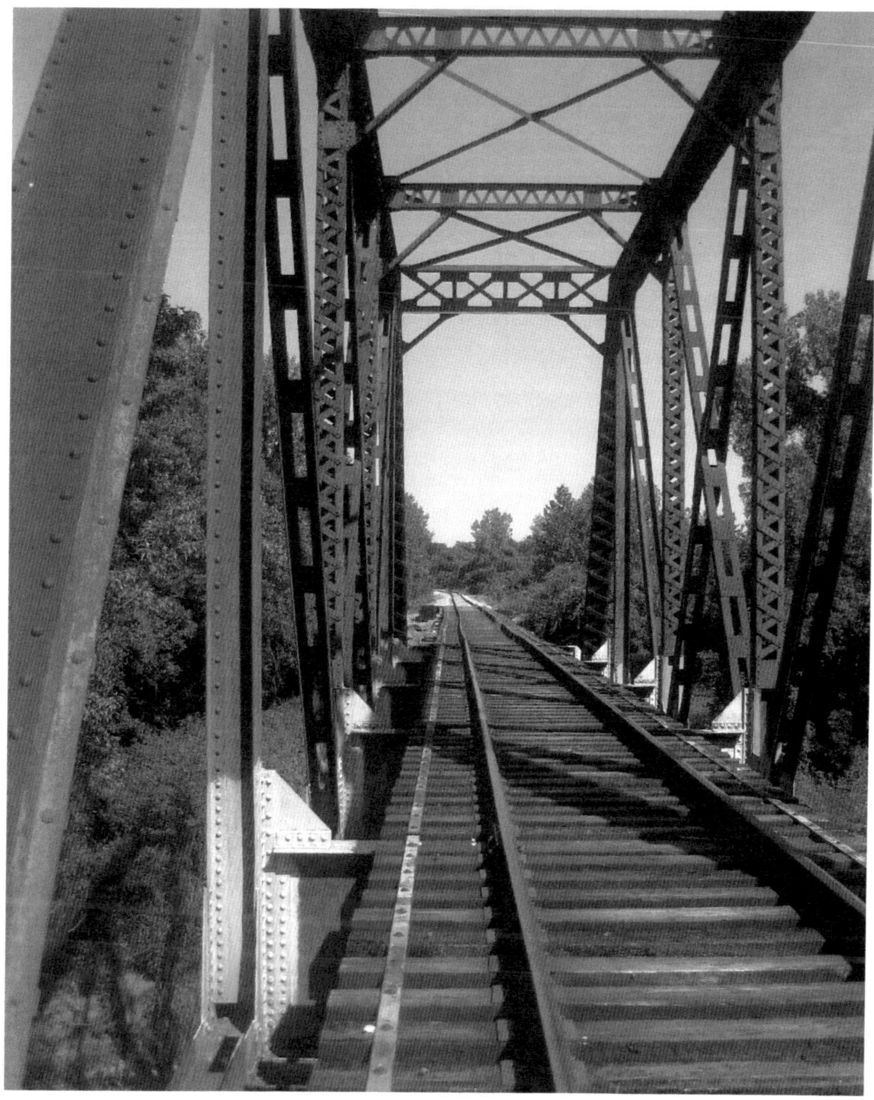

The Tennessee Central Railway bridge spanning White's Creek in Bordeaux was built in 1902. A short distance away, the body of Dorothy Distelhurst was found by two workmen in a shallow grave. *Author's photograph.*

Though Dorothy had probably died shortly after her abduction and certainly hadn't been alive when the notes were sent, the writer had threatened that if Distelhurst did not pay for the release of his daughter, he would "burn her eyes out with acid."[118] Given the evidence at the crime scene, it was a chilling detail that only the killer might have known beforehand.

Beyond that, there was the scant evidence found at the scene, including the probable murder weapons, the box and a man's shirt found nearby. Her lunchbox and clothes were tested for fingerprints, but none could be lifted. All eyes turned to the ransom demands—and then the trail faded. Forensic tests came back confirming that no acid had been used; natural decomposition had accounted for the damage to the body's face. The mysterious letter was just a coincidence. The authorities quite openly admitted they were stumped.

With nothing else to go on, the FBI did the one thing it could in the circumstances. When Distelhurst continued to receive ransom demands well after the discovery of his daughter's remains, they went after the sender with a vengeance. In all, ten letters signed "John" were received in the winter of 1934 claiming Dorothy was alive and well and demanding $50,000 for her release. Evidently, the writer was unaware of the discovery of her body.

Eventually, the feds arrested Alfred Otto Wagner, an ex-con who had done time for kidnapping in New York, and charged him with using the U.S. mail to defraud. Wagner was convicted and locked away for a long time, which at least put a damper on the harassment of the heartbroken family by creeps and lowlifes seeking to cash in on their misery. But it did nothing to solve the murder.

The authorities didn't give up, and the investigation continued, though there was little to go on. For J. Carlton Loser, the case would become something of an obsession that would drag on for the better part of two decades. Loser served as district attorney from 1934 to 1956. Dorothy's disappearance was one of the first cases to cross his desk, and it was one of the few that remained unsolved. He worked for three years to build a case, and when he finally moved in the spring of 1937, the allegations he brought forth were startling indeed.

He charged that W. Lloyd Hamilton, Mrs. Distelhurst's ne'er-do-well brother, was wanted for questioning as a suspect in his own niece's murder. His investigators interviewed a prisoner at Mississippi's Parchman Farm who claimed that Hamilton had confessed to killing the little girl while drunk one night at a party. The prisoner they interviewed had been a deputy sheriff at the time and claimed that Hamilton had been arrested for drunkenness and held for a week at Clarksdale, Mississippi, but that no Nashville officers came to question him and he'd been released. A witness living at the same boardinghouse corroborated the story, and Hamilton's ex-wife said that he'd gotten rid of his car shortly after the murder and that he'd "lost" three shirts soon after the body was found.

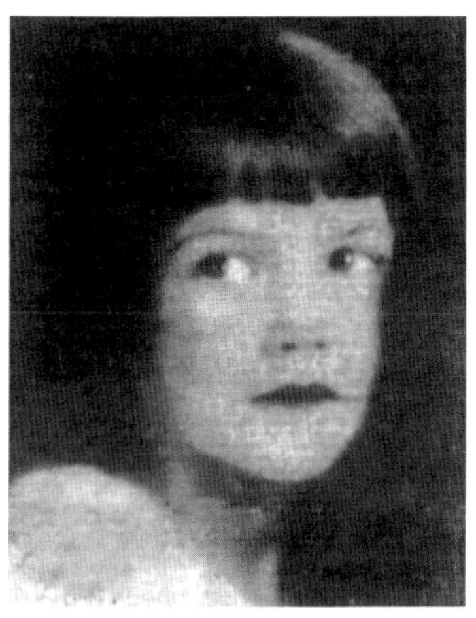

A haunting photograph of Dorothy Distelhurst, who died too soon. *Courtesy Tennessee State Library and Archives.*

Ruby Distelhurst disagreed, calling the tale ridiculous. "I believe the killer is still in this town—waiting to kill somebody else," she said.[119] Hamilton was tracked down in Atlanta and came back to Nashville voluntarily, flatly calling the story a lie. Nonetheless, Loser pressed forward with his investigation, empaneling a grand jury headed up by former FBI agent Joe Towler, who had worked the case after Dorothy disappeared.

The probe dragged through the summer, examining dozens of witnesses. Towler, who appeared to be as haunted by the case as Loser, called in favors with the FBI and the physical evidence was pored over once more. The evidence against Hamilton was circumstantial and no charges were filed against him, but by August, there were tantalizing hints that two new suspects—one a white man, the other African American—were on the verge of being indicted.

And then…nothing.

No charges were filed against the two mystery suspects. The case once more became ice-cold. For two years, things lay dormant before Dorothy's death came back into the headlines in the worst way possible.

On June 15, 1939, twelve-year-old Marian Ellis, known as "Babe" to her friends, left a friend's house to walk to her home on Young's Lane just a quarter of a mile distant. She never made it. The following day, her body was found in a culvert barely ninety yards from her house. She'd been bound, gagged and strangled, then "fiendishly mutilated," according to one report. Tragically, her own brother discovered her body.

Dorothy's case was squarely back in the spotlight as the entire city wondered whether the murders were related. After all, Marian's murder took place only a mile and a half from the spot where Dorothy's body was found five years before. Could a phantom killer have returned after a long hiatus?

As in the earlier case the trail quickly went cold, and it looked like Marian's killer would never be caught. Her family took out a classified ad in the paper every month, announcing "Her Murder Remains

Unsolved," to keep the pressure on the authorities and suspects alike.[120] Their perseverance paid off. In June 1941, Charles Colley was arrested and confessed to her murder, implicating two accomplices. He would eventually be sent to prison for killing Marian, but no evidence was ever found tying him to the Distelhurst case.

And sadly, that was the way it went. Whenever a similar crime occurred, the ghost of little Dorothy Ann came back to haunt the city. There was Jeanette Price, age sixteen, murdered in 1942; Reba Kay Green, fourteen, killed in 1966; Wanda June Anderson, eleven, in 1967; Kathy Jones, twelve, in 1969. In only two cases, those of Jeanette Price and Marian Ellis, was there ever a conviction. Each time it happened, the press dragged up the Distelhurst case, comparing it to the latest tragedy. Then the city quickly forgot and seemed to pretend like it hadn't happened before and would never happen again.

It had and it would, of course, but the years brought no closure to any of them. Even to the case that started it all.

As he prepared to leave office in 1956, Attorney General Loser commented on the case that haunted him, making the eye-opening statement that he was certain that one of three suspects had committed the crime. His unnamed suspects included a "middle-aged businessman…a white collar worker for a Nashville firm" and "a retired construction worker." Over the years of interrogations, these three names had always come up. However, he admitted, he had no evidence to back up his assertions. The men were "one false step away from the electric chair," but he was waiting for them to crack. "The feeling of guilt is timeless. Sometime…that feeling of guilt may give the right man away," he said. He'd done what he could but his wait was in vain, and somehow the thought of a monster who would brutally murder a six-year-old girl having a conscience strikes the modern reader as heartbreakingly naïve.[121]

Unlike fiction, there would be no dramatic confession, no astonishing crack in the case. The most tragic thing about crimes like these, aside from the innocence of the victim, is the frustrating lack of closure. It was a feeling that haunted the Distelhursts for the rest of their lives. And unbelievably, fate had one last cruel twist in store for them.

Their son, Alfred Jr., once wrongly suspected of his half sister's disappearance, continued his wandering life and joined the Merchant Marine at the outbreak of World War II. On January 8, 1943, he was aboard the tanker *Broad Arrow* when it was struck by two torpedoes from *U-124* and exploded off the coast of Suriname. Alfred was among the twenty-three who died that day, his body lost at sea and never recovered. He was twenty-six years old.

Alfred Sr. lived quietly until his death in 1972. Ruby followed him in 1985, and today they lie peacefully beside their daughter who was so savagely taken from them. They lived to see a world where crimes like the one that shattered their lives, once thought so unusual, had become everyday affairs.

If there is one small consolation to take away, it's that we know far more about the nature of these crimes today than we did in 1934. In the decades to come, the FBI would develop strategies for thwarting abductions and psychological profiles of those who perpetrate them. Parents learned to be far more wary, and children were told to be more aware. Multi-state bulletins are immediately issued when a child is endangered. The days of waiting for the ransom demand to come in are long gone, and law enforcement has learned to move as quickly as possible in these situations. New technologies like DNA testing have also cracked open many cold cases, some of which date back fifty years or more. Though too many of these crimes still go unsolved, the chances of catching the perpetrator are far better than they've ever been.

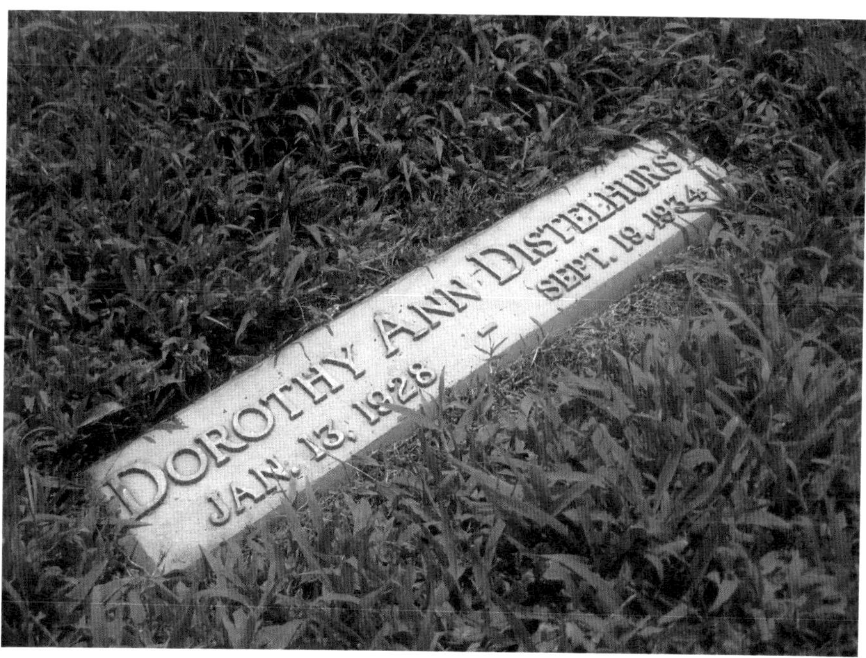

The grave of Dorothy Distelhurst in Woodlawn Cemetery. She lies next to her parents today. *Author's photograph.*

Cold consolation it may be, and it's one that no longer has bearing on Nashville's original sin. The witnesses are long gone, the evidence lost, destroyed or deteriorated. Despite the new advances, there is almost no chance that the murder of Dorothy Ann Distelhurst will ever be solved. In life, she was remembered by those who knew her as a beautiful, shy child with a bright and happy smile. Today, she's remembered—if she's remembered at all—as a symbol of the city's loss of innocence. Reunited with her parents at last, Dottie rests, peacefully forgotten as the city goes about its business.

Like all cities, Nashville has some dark memories. If there is a tendency to avoid bringing up the past here, one can understand. After all, even after eight decades, it seems some of it is just too painful to dwell on.

CHAPTER 12

INTO THIN AIR

The grim days of the Great Depression saw a marked upswing in crime. The one place in town where business seemed to be booming was the Tennessee State Prison. Many hard characters passed through its gates and many deeds were done here, most of which would never see the light of day. It's a place full of mysteries, but none so strange as the story of a small-time punk from Chattanooga who seemingly pulled off the perfect escape. That is, until he sprang back into the headlines twenty years later in a most puzzling fashion.

The central figure in the drama was a skinny kid from Chattanooga named Paul Joe Payne. Payne went wrong early on, and by the time he was a teenager, he was already a seasoned hellraiser, which eventually landed him a one-way ticket to one of the most feared institutions in the state.

Few people today remember the State Training School for Boys, which once hovered just north of Nashville on the Ashland City Highway in the tiny community of Jordonia. Despite its rather innocuous name, it was a reform school where juvenile offenders too young for prison were sent to learn a trade and be rehabilitated. The facility handled kids from their early teens to the age of twenty-one, accused of everything from vandalism and shoplifting to armed robbery and assault with intent to kill. Conditions were harsh, and beatings were frequently handed out. "Being sent to Jordonia" was a threat to be taken seriously, even by tough young incorrigibles like Payne. The abuse and harsh discipline would harden him, as it did many others, and he would learn from older kids how to be a full-blown criminal by the time he was released.

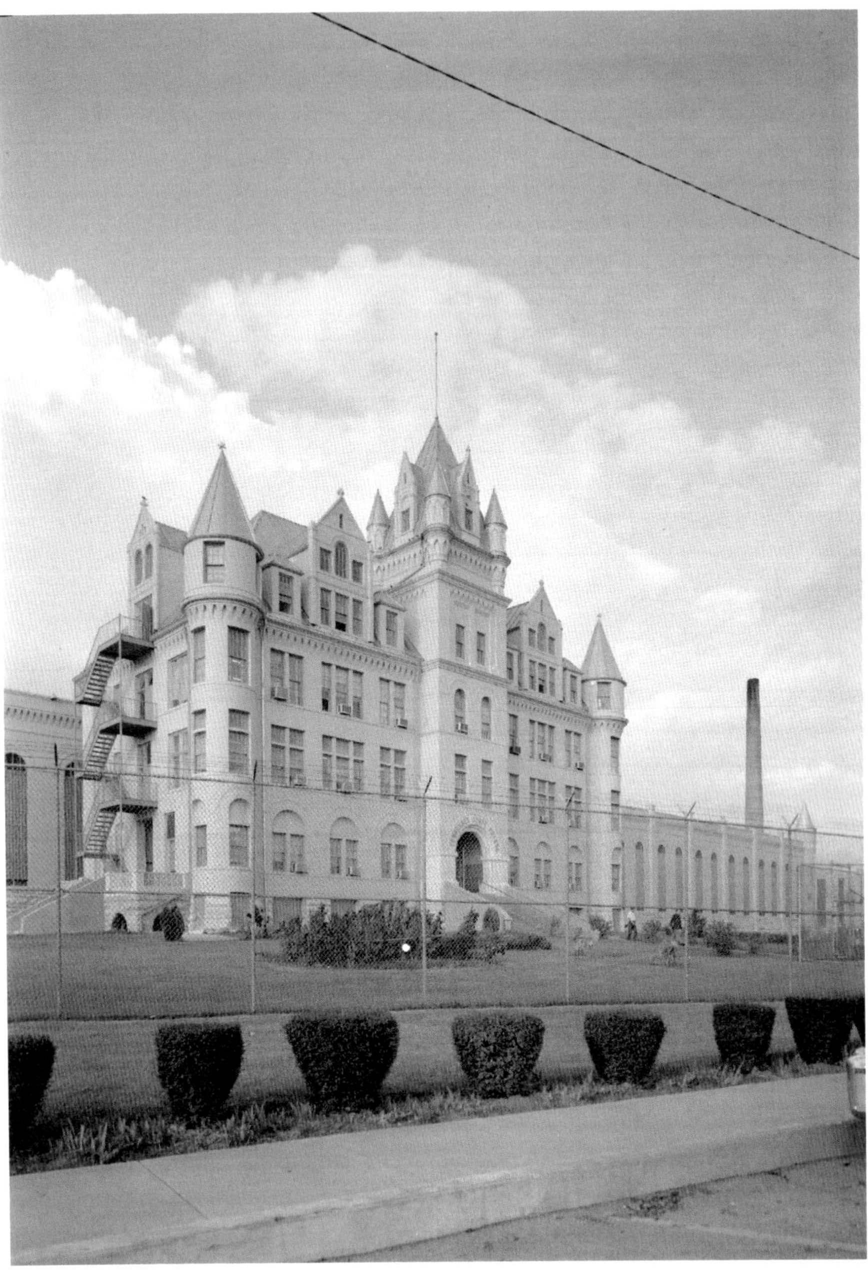

The Tennessee State Prison, site of one of the most bizarre missing persons cases in the state's history. *Library of Congress.*

Payne was unremarkable except for one trait: he was difficult to hold onto. His first recorded escape happened when he was still at Jordonia. He and three others broke out on April 10, 1936, stealing a car from a woman who lived nearby and making their way to Carthage, where they were captured the following evening. The next day, Sheriff Lillard D. Yeaman of Smith County borrowed a car and put the boys in the back for the trip back to Nashville. Evidently, he took the job lightly and underestimated his charges, as he never even bothered to handcuff them.

He also seems to have forgotten that, unlike a police cruiser, his borrowed car had door handles on the inside. As he slowed down to drive around the traffic circle on Public Square, Payne made his move, and all four boys tumbled out of the moving car before fleeing into the alleys of downtown Nashville. Luckily, some nearby police officers gave chase, and three of the boys were quickly recaptured and lodged in the holding cells at the police station. But Payne managed to give them the slip.

A year later, Payne was back in the headlines for a much more serious reason. On his eventual return to Jordonia, he fell in with two truly hard-bitten individuals. Dick Flannery and Chester Johnson, both from Chicago, were only seventeen years old, but they were already seasoned beyond their years. They had been part of a gang that staged a holdup of a Memphis drugstore in 1936. Caught by the cops near Brownsville shortly afterward, they shot it out until they ran out of ammunition and were captured. The third member of their crew, fifteen-year-old Jimmy Magid, shot himself to avoid returning to custody. They escaped from Jordonia on September 7, 1937, along with Payne and two others, and immediately went on a spectacular ten-day crime spree.

Armed with handguns and leaving a trail of stolen cars behind them, the gang staged stickups and strong-arm robberies through Tennessee, Alabama, Georgia, Texas and Illinois. Their youthful faces led to the gang being nicknamed the "Baby Bandits."

On September 15, they decided to take it to the next level. Apparently acting on a tip from Payne and the other Chattanooga boys in their outfit, they pulled up in front of the Industrial Credit Union bank in that city in a stolen car. John Callis, age sixteen, and John Jennings, nineteen, walked inside with drawn pistols and demanded that the cashier raise his hands.

They had picked on the wrong guy. Cashier W.G. Smith dove under the counter and grabbed his own pistol, firing it wildly as the two would-be bandits made a beeline back to their car and disappeared.

Immediately, an APB went out, and officers from three states alongside "scores of well-armed farmers" in improvised posses began a search for the suspects.[122] Two days later, the boys were surrounded in a farmhouse outside Rossville, Georgia. Faced with an army of trigger-happy locals and cops, the boys reportedly hid in the corner of one room, "shaking like leaves,"[123] while the owners of the house negotiated with the police not to fire. When officers entered the house, they meekly surrendered, submitting to the handcuffs despite the fact that they still had revolvers stuffed in their belts. Also arrested was a female accomplice, only fifteen years old, who acted with a lot more resolve. She was photographed calmly smoking and reading a magazine after her capture.

The Baby Bandits had gone too far this time. Jennings, the leader of the bunch, told his junior mob that "they'll send you kids back to the reformatory, but me and Paul will get the walls."[124] He was quite right. This time, they were tried as adults.

Paul Joe Payne, now nineteen years old, was convicted of attempted bank robbery in a Hamilton County court and sentenced to five years. On November 3, 1937, he entered the Brushy Mountain State Penitentiary in Petros, Tennessee, as convict number 30948. He was assigned to the backbreaking task of digging coal for the state in the nearby prison mines.

The following year, his mother died, and Payne was given a pass to attend her funeral. Afterward, he was transferred to the Main Prison facility in Nashville. Perhaps he thought himself a hardened con by this time, but the truth is he was entering into the most dangerous place he'd ever been, and the Baby Bandit was ill equipped to cope with it.

Also doing time at that point was an older, rougher fellow from Woodbury, Tennessee. Taft Fuller had been convicted of the robbery of the Citizens' State Bank at Morrison on the stifling afternoon of July 26, 1933. Fuller, who was 22 at the time, had been the getaway driver but was drunk and slumped behind the wheel when the shooting broke out. It turns out that someone had tipped the authorities off that the bank would be hit, and a local doctor named J.A. Clark tried to arrest him. Fuller killed him with a shotgun blast, but Clark's return fire put fourteen buckshot into his body. The wounded robber and his accomplices were sentenced to a whopping 119 years behind bars for bank robbery and murder.

On the inside, Fuller quickly learned the golden rule. "Tend to your own business," he would later say. "Know nothing, see nothing, and hear nothing. I've never said anything about what I've seen out there, because it wasn't my business. People who tend to other people's business don't live long out there."[125] It was a lesson that Payne didn't take to heart. And years later, his story and Fuller's would collide in a most surprising manner.

The cocky young Payne was doing everything wrong and making enemies right and left. He turned out to be a great gambler. Though gambling was forbidden, it was widely practiced in the dark corners of the shops and the yard, and Payne amassed quite a pile from shooting craps, often as much as several hundred dollars at one time. After his mother's death, he had also come into an inheritance of $6,000, and it seems that he was often seen flashing wads of cash around the cellblock. A prisoner holding that much money without the proper connections was in a very bad situation.

Worse yet, a rumor began floating that Payne had become the one thing that was most despised in that place: a rat. The prison had a flourishing black market, and anything could be had for the right price. Drugs were an increasingly popular escape from such a hopeless world, and the "dope rings" constantly smuggled in opium, heroin, cocaine and other substances from underworld contacts on the outside. Rumor had it that Payne had ingratiated himself with one of the outfits selling the stuff and was offering to sell his knowledge to the authorities in exchange for leniency or even a reduction of sentence.

It may or may not have been true, but in such a paranoid environment, it didn't take much to put a target on one's back. Perhaps Payne sensed the whispering behind his back, perhaps not.

And then one day…he up and vanished. It was September 2, 1939—the day after World War II started. It happened with no trace, leaving prison officials flabbergasted. The last reported sighting of him had him standing in the yard at the recreation break, smoking a cigarette and chatting with a few pals. It wasn't until evening roll call that he was even missed, and then the place was turned upside down searching for him. There was no sign.

Seriously embarrassed, prison officials quietly put out a bulletin to be on the lookout for the escapee while they leaned on informants to find out what happened.

A rumor surfaced that Payne had been murdered for the money he carried and dumped into the swimming pool. The pool was drained and searched, but no sign of foul play was found there—or anywhere else. Reluctantly, administration decided that Payne had pulled off the perfect escape, and they sought to find out how.

One rumor was that he had quietly donned civilian clothing and joined a group of reporters who happened to be touring the prison that day. An official investigation decided that he had hitched a ride on the daily trash

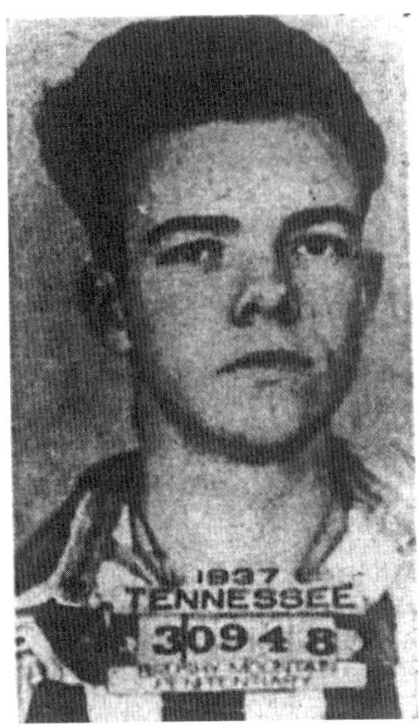

Paul Joe Payne. His disappearance in 1939 set off a wave of speculation about how he could vanish so completely from a maximum-security prison. *Courtesy Tennessee State Library and Archives.*

wagon that hauled refuse out through the front gates. Trash collection was overhauled, security was tightened, a report was submitted to the governor—and that's where they hit a dead end.

The missing man made no contact with his family or friends on the outside. He didn't surface in another harebrained crime spree in another state. He didn't turn up in another prison under an assumed name. It was as if Paul Payne had walked completely off the face of the earth that day.

A few years later, Pearl Harbor was attacked, and with the country at war, there was little time to waste on the search for a small-time crook. But the mystery still nagged as the years went on. How did Payne manage to vanish so completely, and how could they prevent it happening again?

The rumor mill in the prison had its own answers. "One rumor went around that his body had been thrown into a huge hot water tank near the powerhouse," recalled inmate Horace Woodruff. "The tank was drained, but it disclosed no body. Another rumor had it that his body had been thrown into the powerhouse furnace."[126] In 1950, on the eleventh anniversary of his disappearance, a detail went through the ashes in the furnace, but no human remains of any kind were found.

The authorities were more convinced than ever that Payne had walked out somehow and joined the army, disappearing into the sea of GIs who went off to fight. Photographs and fingerprint records were distributed to police departments and government agencies, but still no sign was found. Payne joined the roster of other convicts who had gotten away scot free.

It wasn't impossible, especially for a small timer, and he wasn't alone. In 1944, serial stickup artist J.H. Carne had been a trustee. He told the authorities one afternoon that he had to go on an errand. He never returned. Way back in 1929, Homer Block had walked away from a work detail six months into a one-year sentence for involuntary manslaughter. He was never recaptured. Two decades later, the warden wondered to a reporter,

"I wonder if he often wishes he'd stayed around that extra half year. Six months more in prison is a big price to pay for 21 years of uneasiness."[127]

Presumably, Homer would have disagreed.

Then in 1958, nineteen years after Payne disappeared, his story came back into the spotlight once more.

It started when an unnamed informant spoke to the police chief of Berry Hill about the case on condition of strict anonymity. An internal investigation was launched, and several inmates who were in the prison at the time Payne vanished were questioned. Eventually, three of them agreed to give statements as long as they were put in protective custody. The story they told was cold-blooded.

In the fall of 1939, a new floor was being laid in the prison metal shop, and that's where Payne met several other inmates for a game of craps. One of them, Dick West, was a truly scary fellow, known to carry a knife and use it without compunction. After some time playing, West suddenly accused Payne of being a snitch and then pulled his blade and tried to cut the young bandit. As they wrestled for the knife, convicted robber Jack Youngblood ran into the restroom, grabbed a towel and slipped it around Payne's neck, strangling him to death. When questioned by the others, West claimed he'd received a "package" of drugs recently and that Payne had reported it to prison officials.

After the killing, Youngblood and West dug a shallow grave in the dirt where the concrete slab had been pulled up and stuffed the body into it. Two days later, a work detail that included the two killers poured a new slab on top of the body, sealing it into the floor. It had been the perfect crime, and the best part was that Payne was blamed for escaping.

It made for an interesting story, but there was only one way to confirm it. Prison officials descended upon the metal shop with jackhammers and shovels. And there, just where the informants said it would be, they found what they were looking for.

A human skull grinned up at them from the dirt.

Forensic examination established that the remains were those of a man of about twenty-one years of age, of Payne's size. Immediately, the officials swung into action to track down the killers. They soon hit a snag.

Dick West was already dead after finally biting off more than he could chew. A convicted murderer, West had reportedly beaten his grandmother to death and robbed her of a small amount of money. In his years in prison, he had knifed two other inmates in cellblock fights. Then, on August 10, 1951, he picked on Hermie Lee Jones, who was just as rough as he was. In the fight

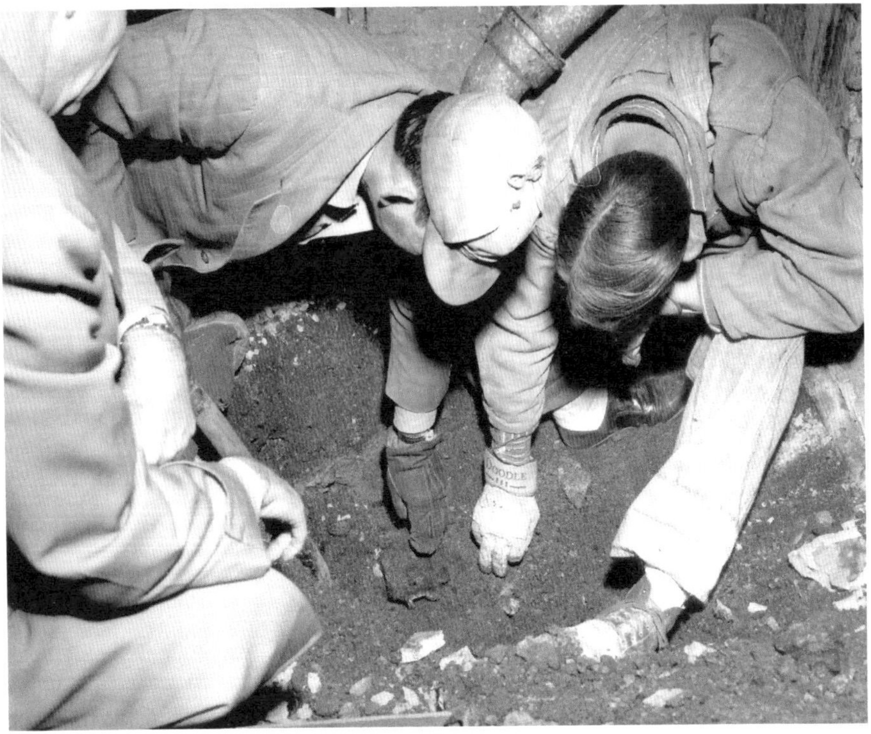

The discovery of the body. Just under the workman's glove in the center can be seen the skull at the center of the mystery. *Nashville Banner Collection, Nashville Public Library Special Collections.*

that followed, Jones killed West, and due to West's prior record, the killing was ruled self-defense.

Jack Youngblood had been paroled in 1940, six months after allegedly strangling Payne. He had joined the U.S. Army Air Corps during the war and served in the Pacific as a B-24 gunner. He was granted a medical discharge and settled in Detroit after his return. As it so happened, Youngblood had just been picked up there on a charge of child molestation. Michigan authorities were advised that he was wanted for questioning in Tennessee. When asked for comment, Youngblood admitted he'd known Payne years ago but claimed that he'd never even gambled with him. He agreed to return to Tennessee, saying, "I don't feel like I have a damn thing to worry about."[128]

A grand jury was empaneled to look into the matter and got off to a promising start. After all, they had a corpse and three witnesses who agreed in their testimony. The problem, as it turned out, was with the remains.

First off, though the witnesses agreed that Payne had been strangled, the skeleton disagreed. The medical examiner found that the cause of death was actually a fractured skull over the right eye, contradicting the witnesses. Then the prison dentist testified that the skull didn't show the signs of some dental work that he'd performed on Payne before he disappeared. The prison records confirmed his testimony, and the dentist told the jury, "I don't see how it could possibly be the same person." In addition, at least one ex-prisoner testified that Payne had borrowed fifty dollars from him the day before he vanished, saying the money was a payoff to allow him to slip through a side gate. Why the man agreed to give the normally wealthy Payne fifty dollars without any chance of getting it back was left unstated.

Youngblood was convicted in Detroit and sentenced to three years. Authorities there informed Tennessee officials that they could have him back if he was indicted for murder, but he never was. The evidence wasn't strong enough, and no true bill was handed down in the case. Officially, the remains were never even identified as Payne's. To this day, his prison record simply reads: "Escaped, 9-2-39."

It's unclear what happened to the mysterious bones after that. Whether they were buried or whether they still sit on an evidence shelf gathering dust is hard to say. If it had happened today, DNA would probably have solved the mystery immediately, but eighty years on there are still lingering questions. It seems clear that Paul Payne must have been murdered in prison, but there are significant reasons to doubt the skeleton found in the metal shop was his. Then again, if they weren't his bones, then whose were they?

As it turned out, the prison was very good at making people disappear. In fact, one of them was standing right there in plain sight.

Taft Fuller, the convicted Morrison bank robber, garnered quite a bit of attention in the aftermath of the hearing. He was one of those playing dice in the shop when the alleged murder took place and testified before the grand jury, though he said he left before Payne was actually killed. Fuller became a minor celebrity when it turned out that he'd not had a visitor or a letter in fifteen years. He had no friends or family and no supporters to plead his case before the parole board. He was, as the press dubbed him, the "Forgotten Man" of the prison.

He recalled that Payne's murder was one of twenty-five he'd personally seen or heard of during his time inside. He said that he'd lived "in hell for 25 years," and when asked what he'd do if he was released, he replied, "Anybody would be a fool to let the same dog bite him twice." A groundswell of support grew for Fuller's cause, and gifts and offers of sponsorship poured in. In 1961, he was finally granted parole and left the prison a free man.

However, the dog that he feared turned out to be a hound on his trail, and one he couldn't outrun. Like many former prisoners, Fuller couldn't seem to shake his demons. He would be in and out of prison throughout the 1960s for parole violation, usually stemming from his alcoholism. In 1971, he was paroled for the final time and boarded a bus to start a new life in Texas.

Then on February 6, 1974, a trailer home in McMinnville, Tennessee, went up in flames. Days later, firefighters found human remains in the ashes. The body was eventually identified as Taft Fuller, who had recently returned to Tennessee. A .32-caliber handgun was found near his body, but it was unfired, and there was no sign of trauma on the remains. The cause of death was unclear, but ultimately it was not ruled foul play. He was buried quietly afterward, forgotten to the end. He was sixty-five years old.

He took with him the truth about the mysterious skeleton beneath the floor that turned out to be both a blessing and a curse for him. Was it really Paul Payne or was it someone else? And did he know more than he told about the events that ended in murder that day? It's frustrating but maybe oddly fitting that we end on this note. We all love a good mystery after all.

And as we've seen, Nashville has plenty of secrets, and it guards them well.

NOTES

Chapter 1

1. *Boston Post*, October 6, 1840.
2. Thomas, *From Tennessee Slave*, 58–59.
3. Ibid.
4. *Republican Banner*, January 20, 1843.
5. Seals, *History of White County.*
6. Humphreys, *Reports of Cases Argued in the Supreme Court of Tennessee*, 289.
7. Ibid.
8. Haynes, *Lives and Confessions.*
9. Ibid.
10. Ibid.
11. Ibid.

Chapter 2

12. *Union and American*, February 1, 1874.
13. Ibid.
14. *Memphis Daily Appeal*, March 19, 1874.
15. *Union and American*, March 21, 1874.
16. Ibid., April 29, 1874.
17. *Daily American*, October 23, 1883.

18. *Daily Union*, November 1, 1883.
19. Ibid.
20. Ibid., November 1, 1883.
21. Ibid., November 14, 1883.
22. Ibid., November 22, 1884.
23. Ibid., November 30, 1884.
24. *Tennessean*, April 5, 1927.

Chapter 3

25. Lyon, *Wild, Wild West*, 82.
26. Yeatman, *Frank and Jesse James*, 151.
27. *Daily American*, April 19, 1882
28. Yeatman, *Frank and Jesse James*.
29. *Daily American*, December 25, 1904.
30. Croy, *Cole Younger.*
31. Yeatman, *Frank and Jesse James*, 227.
32. Ibid., 240.

Chapter 4

33. *Daily American*, January 27, 1891.
34. Ibid.
35. Ibid., January 31, 1891.
36. Ibid., February 2, 1891.
37. Ibid., January 31, 1891.
38. Ibid., February 2, 1891.
39. Ibid., September 24, 1891.
40. Ibid., September 25, 1891.
41. Ibid.
42. *Banner*, September 24, 1891.
43. *Daily American*, September 24, 1891.
44. *Banner*, January 31, 1891.

105. *Tennessean*, April 11, 1934.
106. Ibid.
107. King, *Rise and Fall of the Dillinger Gang*, 166.
108. FBI Dillinger Gang File, Report of SAC E.J. Connelley, September 13, 1935.

Chapter 10

109. Convict Record, Rufus Guy, Tennessee State Penitentiary.
110. *Tennessean*, December 21, 1977.
111. *Banner*, March 8, 1934.
112. *Tennessean*, March 8, 1934.
113. *Banner*, March 19, 1934.
114. *Tennessean*, December 21, 1977.

Chapter 11

115. *Tennessean*, September 23, 1934.
116. *Banner*, September 23, 1934.
117. Ibid.
118. *Tennessean*, November 16, 1934.
119. Ibid., April 15, 1937.
120. Ibid., June 26, 1941.
121. Ibid., December 30, 1956.

Chapter 12

122. *Times*, September 16, 1937.
123. *Tennessean*, September 18, 1937.
124. Ibid.
125. Ibid., March 20, 1958.
126. Woodroof, *Stone Wall College*, 136.
127. *Tennessean*, October 30, 1950.
128. Ibid., February 22, 1958.

BIBLIOGRAPHY

Books

Croy, Homer. *Cole Younger, Last of the Great Outlaws*. Lincoln, NE: Bison Books, 1999.

Ernst, Donna B. *Women of the Wild Bunch*. Souderton, PA: Wild Bunch Press, 2004.

Haynes, Milton. *Lives and Confessions of Zebediah Payne, Willis Green Carroll, and Archibald Kerby*. Nashville: Republican Banner Office, 1843.

Humphreys, West H. *Reports of Cases Argued and Determined in the Supreme Court of Tennessee, 1843–4*. Nashville: Republican Banner Office, 1844.

King, Jeffery S. *The Rise and Fall of the Dillinger Gang*. Nashville: Cumberland House, 2005.

Lynch, Sylvia. *Harvey Logan in Knoxville*. College Station, TX: Early West, 1998.

Lyon, Peter. *The Wild, Wild West*. New York: Funk & Wagnalls, 1969.

Seals, Monroe. *History of White County, Tennessee*. N.p.: privately printed, 1935.

Smokov, Mark T. *He Rode with Butch and Sundance*. Denton: University of North Texas Press, 2012.

Thomas, James. *From Tennessee Slave to St. Louis Entrepreneur*. Columbia: University of Missouri Press, 1984.

Woodroof, Horace M. *Stone Wall College*. Nashville: Aurora Publishers, 1970.

Yeatman, Ted P. *Frank and Jesse James: The Story Behind the Legend*. Nashville: Cumberland House, 2000.

Newspapers

Banner (Nashville, TN)
Daily American (Nashville, TN)
Daily Appeal (Memphis, TN)
Daily News (Nashville, TN)
Daily News Journal (Murfreesboro, TN)
Evening Sun-Democrat (Paducah, KY)
Globe (Nashville, TN)
Microfilm Collections, Tennessee State Library and Archives, Nashville, TN.
Post-Dispatch (St. Louis, MO)
Tennessean (Nashville, TN)
Times (Kingsport, TN)
Union and American (Nashville, TN)

Official Records

Case Files, Tennessee Supreme Court. Tennessee State Library and Archives, Nashville.

Federal Bureau of Investigation. Reports on John Dillinger and Gang. Accessed online at vault.fbi.gov/John%20Dillinger%20.

Inmate Records, Tennessee State Prison. Record Group 25. Tennessee State Library and Archives, Nashville.

INDEX

ABOUT THE AUTHOR

A lifelong native of Nashville, Brian Allison comes by his interest in the city's past naturally. He has worked for more than twenty years in the field of public history at museums such as Travellers Rest and the Hermitage. He has worked in film and appeared on television as a guest speaker for shows like the History Channel's *America's Secret Slang* and *Blood and Fury* for the American Heroes Channel. He is also the author of *Murder and Mayhem in Nashville*, released by The History Press in 2016.